MW01050721

Last Call For Help

Changing North America One Teen at a Time

Dayle Maloney
&
Dawson McAllister

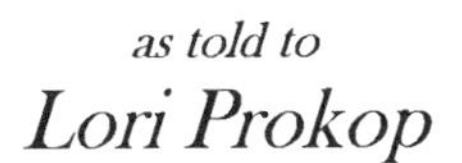

as told to
Lori Prokop

Williams & Wilson
International Press

Privacy Statement

The circumstances, details and names of the teenagers in the stories contained within this book have been changed to protect the privacy of the families involved.

Acknowledgements

Thanks to the teenagers and their families who so bravely shared their stories so readers can experience the benefits of the HopeLine.

Thanks to the HopeLine staff for helping North America's youth. You are an extremely talented group of caring Christians.

Thanks to all the people who have donated their hearts, time and financial resources to provide North America's young people with the HopeLine.

Thanks to David Bertrand, Jana Mitcham, and the distributors of Nutrition For Life International for your support of the HopeLine.

Thanks to Paul Ramseyer and Neil Stavem of KTIS Radio, Minneapolis/St. Paul for listening to the wants of young people. It was through KTIS that *Dawson McAllister Live!* and the HopeLine were first launched. Also thank you to Northwestern College Productions and Skylight Productions who distribute the HopeLine with the sole purpose of reaching and helping youth. Thanks to our editor Linda Cadwalader Gulbrandson for your focus and commitment to this project. Thanks to Michael Cartwright for a great job on the cover.

To Our Families With Love

The publisher and authors disclaim any warranty, expressed or implied, and shall have neither liability nor responsibility to any person or entity regarding the financial or personal results from the use of the methods, advice, systems or information contained in this book. Every effort has been made to change the circumstances and names of the people and families contained within the stories presented in this book. Every effort has been made to make this text as complete as possible. However, there may be some mistakes both typographical and in content. Therefore, this text should only be used as a general guide and not as the ultimate source of information. This text and/or the Dawson McAllister HopeLine are not meant to replace medical or other professional services.

First Printing 1999

How To Order

Single and multiple copies may be ordered from:
Dayle Maloney & Associates, Ltd., 3301 Golf Road, Eau Claire, Wisconsin, 54701 (800)457-6588 or (800)621-2065.

Contents

PART 1: Last Call For Help 9

CHAPTER 1: Hope Begins With The Person Who Believes In You 11

PART 2: The Best Inheritance A Parent Can Give Is Time And Love *29*

CHAPTER 2: We Can Do More Than Care; We Can Help 31

CHAPTER 3: Opening The HopeLine 24 Hours A Day, 7 Days A Week, 365 Days A Year 40

CHAPTER 4: The Company With A Cause 45

CHAPTER 5: A Hero In Every Heart 50

CHAPTER 6: There Is More To Life Than Having Everything 56

CHAPTER 7: Teens Want Time With Parents 66

CHAPTER 8: What Can Parents Expect From The HopeLine? 74

CHAPTER 9: It's Not Over 'Til It's Over 78

PART 3: Teenagers Are Crying Out 83

CHAPTER 10: Are Kids Struggling More Today? 85

CHAPTER 11: The Evolution Of Teens 90

CHAPTER 12: Who's Loving Our Kids? 96

CHAPTER 13: High School Horror 108

CHAPTER 14: Dealing With Shame 118

CHAPTER 15: Taking The Time To Listen 120

CHAPTER 16: Volunteering For The Kids 122

CHAPTER 17: Showing Kids The Light 124

PART 4: Pain Relief For Your Soul 127

CHAPTER 18: When Teens Talk, We Listen 129

CHAPTER 19: $5 Saves A Life 140

CHAPTER 20: Kids Want Help 142

PART 5: Lessons From Littleton 145

CHAPTER 21: Teens Teach The World 147

CHAPTER 22: Is My School Next? 149

CHAPTER 23: If They Only Had One Friend 152

CHAPTER 24: People Don't Care How Much You Know Until They Know How Much You Care 155

CHAPTER 25: Teens Claim God's Promise 159

CHAPTER 26: Which Path Will You Take? 162

CHAPTER 27: I Feel Their Pain 165

CHAPTER 28: You Make A Living By What You Receive; You Make A Life By What You Give 168

I Want To Help The Kids 172

PART 1

Last Call For Help

CHAPTER 1

Hope Begins With The Person Who Believes In You

Sleet slapped her face creating tiny welts on her skin. She was unaware of the pain. It didn't matter. Soon her suffering would be over.

Chills ran up her spine as her tennis shoes kicked dirt and rocks sitting loosely on top of the frozen gravel road. It was as if they were challenging her, "I dare you to kick me." Up to this point, figuratively, Sarah hadn't kicked much. She still smoked, even though her mother said 14-year-olds were too young for cigarettes. And there was her boyfriend, Dave. Sarah was sure he would start to hit the baby, now an 8-week fetus, just like he did

Sarah. "If you wouldn't make me so mad. If you weren't so stupid. If you stopped looking at other guys." He assured her that he would stop hitting her if she was able to behave like his last girlfriend.

But her mom tolerated the same thing. Sarah witnessed her father's countless attacks on her mother. They fermented a sick feeling in the pit of Sarah's stomach which defied gravity and made its way to the back of Sarah's throat. She could taste its bitterness even now as her mind's eye replayed the assaults. Lately, the violence at home was becoming more than she could take — morning sickness at school and gut-wrenching fear when the family was together at night. The pain grew with no end in sight.

Sarah had stewed on her decision long and hard for the last year. No one knew that for months she had toyed with the idea of ending it all as her pain rose and subsided like the red mercury of a thermometer. As of late, her situation had heated to an extreme.

"School," she thought. "No one will miss me, and if they do, they'll get over it." Her math teacher had reprimanded her in front of the class about an assignment Sarah lost the night her father turned his rage on her. The teen used her school duffel bag to shield her body. It was only a slight inconvenience for her father who ripped it from her hands, tearing and destroying the contents. Humiliation instilled by her family made Sarah certain she would have to lie in school to cover the truth. "Every family has its secrets," was the silent message communicated through her mother's tear-filled eyes.

As with most adolescents, Sarah couldn't see past her teenage years. She had no idea that in just 24 months her life would change. School graduation. New boyfriend. Her father would soon be gone. Sarah had fallen into an unforgiving depression with no idea how to escape. The pain held her mind captive, controlling her thoughts.

A car drove by and road slush hit Sarah's face. She didn't try to avoid it. "What's it matter? It'll be washed off soon enough by the icy, cold water of the river," Sarah muttered as tears began to solidify on her numbing purplish-red cheeks. It was 16 degrees and Sarah had left her coat at home. "Why take a perfectly good coat to the bottom of the river with me?" she taunted. "Maybe Mom can get some money for it." Her parents were having financial difficulties since the company her father worked for had down-sized and laid off most of the senior managers. He took a job delivering for the local feed mill. Every week Sarah's family sold a little more to keep the wolves from the door. "Let them in," Sarah mused. "Maybe we could eat *them* and Dad would lighten up on Mom about spending money on food." Times were tough for Sarah.

Playing back the thoughts of her family made her all the more certain she was making the right decision for her and her baby. Her father would kill her or worse beat her within an inch of her life while humilating and then disowning her. He had a way of shredding people with his piercing eyes and sharp tongue. Surviving his attack would be torturous.

Yes, she had gone to a family counselor as well as the youth minister at her church. The youth minister befriended her and gave her direction, but he was too close to the family to confide all her secrets. Everyone knew everyone. The family counselor was from another town, but to Sarah he might as well have been from another planet. She instantly sized him up as a total "dork" with no clue about teens. He could probably comfort her grandmother, God rest her soul, during baking days upon the rare instance when one of her cakes would fall, but Sarah's problems? Get real. She didn't trust him at all.

What would the town think after Sarah was gone? "It could be anyone's kid," Sarah reasoned. She wasn't the only one ready to end it all. Her friends Nikki and Greg had already attempted with pills and alcohol. Their parents didn't know. It happened at parties where other kids intervened. They made Nikki puke and talked Greg out of taking the pills he held in his hand. Sarah was there both times with about 30 other kids. Teens have their secrets, too. That was months ago and no parent had ever found out.

"Parents think they know everything about their teens but they don't know the half of it," Sarah mouthed with disgust. Any young person can tell you that in addition to selective hearing, kids also practice selective talking. "My daughter tells me everything," Sarah mimed sarcastically as she thought of the conversation she overheard her mother having with the women at church. The other women nodded in agreement affirming that they also knew everything about their teens' lives.

"Fat chance," Sarah sneered in pain. "What teen would stoop as low as going to their parents for help. That's like holding up the white flag to the enemy. It's my parents who are causing this mess," Sarah reasoned. "Besides, they never really listen." Every teenager that Sarah knew agreed that while parents were there for some things, never trust them with everything.

To even talk to parents, Sarah and her friends have to use a foreign language that is dull and full of judgement. And every kid knows that confiding in parents will result in a lecture, a grounding or a drama equal to anything you find on TV soap operas. "Parents blow everything out of proportion," Sarah shook her head and sighed.

Like years ago when her brother Mike was caught with a knife to his throat, she remembered. Her parents went nuts. They forbid the family to talk about it. They went with Mike to the youth counselor at church.

"Mike's problem stems from the time his teacher reprimanded him, his father scolded him and he was picked last for the softball team." Sarah recalled she and Mike listened to the three adults in the church office referring to the suicide attempt. Sarah remembered her eyes darting to Mike who painfully looked at her as if to say, "These idiots can't even talk about the truth. See why suicide was the way to go? They are so out of touch with reality." The truth was Sarah's parents were saving themselves and losing their children.

"Denial is not a river in Egypt," Sarah thought as she continued her two mile walk to the bridge.

Shortly after the church counseling session, Sarah gathered the courage to ask her father if he thought the family had any problems which might have caused Mike's decision. The only thing sharper than her father's eyes was the tone of his words: "That's none of your business, Sarah. Eat your food and be damn glad you have it. There are starving kids right here in America who don't have it as good as you or Mike."

Last Call For Help

Sarah asked her mom if the family was going to figure out how to get along. "Oh, honey, no family is perfect. That's why Mike has his counselor to talk to if he wants. We don't fight anymore than anyone else. Your father is under a lot of pressure at work. He can't help blowing up at us. But, *you* could help by getting better grades, burning those jeans with holes in them and getting rid of your friends who your dad doesn't like."

When Sarah asked, "Mom, how would you feel if Mike were gone?" the answer was, "Oh, Sarah why do you have to ask these kinds of questions?" Sarah's mother paused and then continued with a sigh, "Yes, our life would be incomplete without Mike. I would have one less child to pick up after and one less to bring home bad grades. Sarah, who knows if he really would have done it, anyway."

Well, they wouldn't have to second-guess Sarah. The cards were dealt and she was holding a bum hand. By now Sarah's vision was blurred by tears. She knew the bridge was close because she could make out the image of Hansen's Service Station. They fixed her family's cars. As Sarah approached the old-fashioned gas station she noticed it was deserted. "Must be after two," she thought. Sarah knew what time they closed on Sundays because she often used the phone in the booth at the end of their lot. She could make a call from there and have complete privacy.

The person who would take her death the hardest would be her brother Mike. Even though he was older, he still depended on her for comfort. Dad was particularly critical of Mike. Sarah could sometimes derail her father's rage by creating an accidental mishap like spilling milk or missing the dishwasher and sending a plate crashing to the floor. Mike did the same for Sarah. Instinctively, they looked out for each other.

She hadn't left a note for Mike. She felt a twang of guilt in her heart. He'd be on his own having to face the family's problems without her. She had thought about how different life would have been if Mike had committed suicide. She was very thankful he was still with her, especially the times he saved her by playing the distraction game.

"I've had enough," she screamed into Hansen's deserted parking lot as the pain broke her. Her knees buckled as she fell to the cement. Her back rested against the phone booth. She gasped for air, tears choking her. Her body convulsed. She couldn't remember living without pain.

Sarah was relieved as her body grew tired. With little energy to struggle in the frigid current of the Mississippi, she hoped drowning in ice-cold water would be like going to sleep. Sarah guessed that it would numb her to a calm and then take her life. As she rose to her feet, the young teen felt obliged to make one last call. Sarah wanted to apologize to Mike, but she knew she couldn't call him directly. He'd do anything to stop her. Mike was a good guy.

Sarah was sheltered from the winter wind as she stood in the phone booth. Her body shook uncontrollably from the change in temperature. The phone booth was at least 10 degrees warmer than outside.

This would be her last call for help. She wanted to do something to lighten the pain for her brother. Her death would be hard on him. She picked up the chilled receiver, which felt warm in her frost-bitten hand, and reached into her pockets only to realize these were clean jeans. She forgot to transfer her change from her other pair. With no money, who could she call for help?

"Just forget it," she screamed deciding the call wouldn't matter anyway.

"Death is death. Everyone goes sooner or later. If I was suddenly hit by a bus, I'd be gone without warning," Sarah shouted rationalizing her own mortality. But, the loyalty she felt for her brother stood beyond the test of reason.

Sarah remembered that Mike had given her the phone number for a place to call if she ever needed help. They sat in her room and memorized it. Mike was into that sort of thing since his suicide attempt. Always have a back-up plan — have somewhere to turn. Sarah thought it was stupid, but she loved Mike enough to support his ideas no matter how strange they seemed.

She remembered sitting on her bed having to recite, "one eight hundred three nine four hope." Over and over, she and Mike recited the number for the HopeLine. Mike made Sarah promise she would call the HopeLine if the need arose and he wasn't around.

In an automatic response to her brother's voice echoing in her mind, she began pushing the buttons on the phone. 1-8-0-0-3-9-4-H-O-P-E.

"HopeLine, this is Jenny," the woman on the other end offered. Sarah was taken off-guard as the phone had rung only once. "Ah, yeah. Well, my brother calls in and I was wondering if you could get him a message?"

"We can help. Who's this?" Jenny asked calmly.

"Well, really I just need to get a message to my brother, " Sarah repeated.

"Where's your brother now?"

"Working."

"Where are you?"

"In a phone booth."

"Does your brother live with you?"

"Yeah, but you're asking too many questions. Just take this message. Tell him...." Sarah paused. How would she give Jenny a message for Mike without revealing her plan? "Tell him...that he's a good brother in a bad situation and that I love him."

"Okay, I got that. Now, what's his name?"

"Mike."

"Okay, what's your name."

She didn't figure it would matter because soon she would be at the bottom of the river. "I'm his sister, Sarah."

"Is something going wrong for Mike?" Jenny asked urging Sarah to continue talking.

"It's going wrong for a lot of people," Sarah generalized.

"Could you tell me about that? I understand bad situations. I've been there myself. It's tough and it hurts, " Jenny slowly continued.

Sarah stopped talking. A wave of pain overtook her. She began to sob uncontrollably.

"I'm here for you, Sarah. I'm here *with* you. Sarah, I care about your pain," Jenny assured her. "Can we talk about it? I'll listen. What we say is private. We don't even know each other, but I do care."

There was a long pause before Sarah exploded, "I hate everything about my life! And I'm going to end it. Don't even try to stop me. Just give this message to my brother Mike and everything will be all right. That's how you can help me."

"You must love your brother if you want to say good-bye to him. What's your brother like?" Jenny asked.

Sarah thought about Mike for a moment before saying, "I know what you're trying to do. You're not going to talk me out of this. The bridge is right over there, so forget it. I'm done with the crap at home. I just feel bad I'm leaving Mike behind. If it wasn't murder, I'd take him with me."

"Sarah, it sounds like your brother is a good guy who needs you. How would he take living without you?" Jenny knew every minute the conversation continued was another minute Sarah was spared from death.

"I can't think about that," Sarah confessed.

"Death is so final. It's a permanent solution to temporary problems. Sarah, tell me what's going on," Jenny urged in a concerned tone.

"These problems are not temporary! This is the only way out!" Sarah screamed.

"Okay, do your parent's know?"

"You've got to be kidding. They *are* my problem," Sarah exploded as the pain of her life flashed through her mind.

"Sounds like things are tough at home. What's going on?"

"You wouldn't understand. No one does. Only Mike and I. That's why he needs this message," Sarah directed firmly. "Will you give it to him?"

"Yes. We have a lot of Mikes who call in here. Could you describe him? What's he like?" asked Jenny.

A legitimate question, Sarah thought. "He's 16 and kinda serious but can be really funny at times. Most of my friends say their brothers are dorks but mine is pretty much okay."

"Sounds like you're close to each other."

"Yeah, he helps me out." Sarah's eyes swelled with tears as she saw Mike's face in her mind's eye.

"How does he do that, Sarah?"

The teen paused, wiping warm tears from her cold face. "Well, my folks fight a lot and Mike and I talk about it. That helps. And if my dad is mad at me, Mike helps me there, too." Sarah's thoughts returned to the last time Mike spilled milk to distract her dad.

"Sarah, you're going to really hurt Mike if you do this. Did you look at all your options before you made this choice?"

"I have no options. That's why I have to do this. Everything is terrible, and it will never get better," Sarah insisted wildly.

"Mmm, since we're talking about Mike and how he loves and needs you, let's look at your options for Mike's sake. He'd want you to do that before you made a final decision. You can't undo death."

Sarah swallowed the lump in her throat. "I'm just tired of it all. There's no end to it. My parents have no clue. I'm tired of trying to be something I'm not."

Jenny could feel a layer between them peel away as Sarah continued. “My grades aren’t good enough. My friends aren’t good enough. My clothes are wrong. Everything I do is wrong. And my boyfriend…” Sarah stopped short. Jenny could feel the sudden pause.

“What’s his name?”

“Dave.”

“How’s it going with Dave?”

“Not so good.”

“Tell me about that.”

“He’s a jerk right now. He’s so possessive. If I even look at another guy he gets mad.”

“How mad?”

“Mad enough”

“Mad enough for what?”

“He’s hit me a few times.”

“A few times?”

“Yeah.”

"Sarah, you don't deserve that. No one does. What would you do if you saw someone hitting a person that you loved?"

"I have. My dad does it all the time to my mom and sometimes Mike and me."

"Sarah, we have to get you and your brother to a safe place. I know some safe places. I can help you. This violence puts you in serious danger. Do you know that you could end up hurt?"

"I know and I'm really worried about...." Sarah paused realizing that she had said too much.

"What worries you the most?"

"I can't say. I can't tell," Sarah said shamefully.

"Sarah, we don't know each other. I'm here in Texas. I'm with you, here to help you. I'm on your side. What else is up?"

Sarah paused as she mustered the courage. She gasped, "I'm pregnant."

"Are you sure?"

"Yes, totally sure."

"Have you decided what you're going to do for the baby?"

Sarah thought for a moment and remembered, "Yeah, I'm going to jump off the bridge. That way we'll both be out of our pain."

"Sarah, your baby is protected inside you. I don't think the baby is in pain but I do know it loves you and wants to live. That's why the baby was conceived. . . to live. Killing yourself would be ending your baby's life. You have other options. Let's talk about them for the life inside you and so your brother can see his niece or nephew. "

Sarah had never thought of her situation that way. . . Mike's niece or nephew, huh?

The conversation fluctuated between peaks and valleys for thirty-three minutes. Finally, Sarah and Jenny reached an agreeable plateau.

"Sarah, will you give me your word that before you hurt yourself you will call us here at the HopeLine?"

Sarah paused knowing what Jenny wanted to hear, "Yes, I promise."

"Sarah, are you going home now?"

Reality hit. Sarah had agreed to live. She had been out in the cold for hours and now it was time to go home.

"All right, I'll give it *one* more try and that's it." Sarah responded half-heartedly, wanting to please Jenny. The teen was not entirely sure she was going to keep that promise.

"You'll call me when you get home? I'll have phone numbers of people who can privately help you and be there for you in your area. They will listen and protect you. And the other HopeLine call managers and I are here for you." Jenny assured her.

"I promise," Sarah said as she rolled her eyes and shook her head. She was annoyed her that her plan was not going to be executed yet slightly relieved.

The conversation was over, but Sarah was sure the insanity would continue. She hung up the phone, opened the door and stepped into the wind. Sarah looked back on her life and tried to make sense of it all. Just two hours earlier she had been hopelessly certain death was her only way out. Her wounds were still fresh as her eyes lifted and followed the dusky outline of the gravel route home. She knew she had a rough road ahead of her. The young girl's heart was darkened with fear and doubt, yet somewhere in her soul Sarah felt an inkling of hope.

PART 2

The Best Inheritance A Parent Can Give Is Time And Love

CHAPTER 2

We Can Do More Than Care; We Can Help

Dawson McAllister

Through the network which we've built here at the HopeLine, Sarah was directed to people who help teens right in her community. Financial arrangements were made so Sarah could receive the guidance she needed without putting a strain on her parents' limited funds.

Gradually, a purpose and meaning manifested in Sarah's life. She left her abusive boyfriend and learned to stay out of bad relationships. Sarah gained the understanding and skills she needed to stay safe and deal effectively with her father's anger and her mother's lack of protection.

Over the course of the last 7 years, Sarah has stayed in touch with the HopeLine. Today, at 21-

years-old, Sarah is in college to advance her future and is the mother of two loved children.

Without the HopeLine, this ending wouldn't have been so happy.

WHAT IS THE HOPELINE?

The HopeLine is a toll-free call center reaching kids in the United States and Canada. Listening and Biblical support and guidance are offered to students 21-years and under by calling 1-800-394-HOPE.

Parents know when their kids call, they will receive Christian values, compassion and understanding. Mom and Dad can't always be there, so we have put this safety net in place to provide comfort for kids and parents.

The HopeLine staff fields calls which vary from serious, immediate concerns such as suicide, abuse and rape to light issues such as "puppy love." Our budget will allow 65,000 kids to receive help. Financial constraints force another 160,000 kids to go without help because they will have called after hours or received a busy signal. In 1999, over 5,000 kids called in one week following the Colorado high school shooting. We estimate next year over 200,000 kids will call for guidance and support.

IN THE BEGINNING

As a spiritual teacher for the past 31 years, I have taught and listened to teens as they have sought a relationship with God. I first developed a connection with young people by traveling through North America presenting weekend conferences. Kids paid $25 to attend. They also received a manual which I wrote specifically for teens about dealing with their feelings. I taught and interacted with anywhere from 10 to 10,000 kids per conference. Since 1968, over 2 million teenagers have attended those weekend events.

The annual growth in the number of kids I worked with presented two major challenges. First, I could not go out into the large audiences and talk with the young people one-on-one because the kids were mobbing me. Secondly, they were hungry for answers, but at best, I visited their town once a year.

In 1989, I began to pray, "How can I talk with these kids individually, or at least so they'll think that I am talking to them individually, every week?" Only God and I knew my desires, but that was more than enough.

In 1990, I became a weekly guest on Don Hawkins' call-in radio show *A Life's Perspectives*. I spoke on the air with parents about the problems they were having with their kids. Soon afterwards, Kirby Anderson of Probe Ministries called and asked me to co-host a call-in radio show for kids.

Subsequently, Skylight Productions and Northwestern College Productions in Minneapolis contacted me to consider guest hosting their radio show *Sunday Night Alive!* In January, 1991, on the evening concluding a weekend youth conference at the Target Center in Minneapolis, I drove over to radio station KTIS and was on the air for two hours. Kids called the show to talk. I listened and offered guidance.

As a result of the success, we decided to launch *Dawson McAllister Live!* which started with ten radio stations.

Not long after the initial accomplishments of the radio ministry, I became dissatisfied with our results. Thousands of teens were trying to get through for help only to hear busy signals. Because of the time constraints of radio and the show airing only two hours, one night a week, even those teens who did get through were limited in the amount of guidance they could receive. I couldn't just say, "Gee, I'm sorry. We've run out of time" to suicidal kids who called the show for help. I knew my audience was frustrated. I was certainly frustrated.

The idea came to offer an off-the-air phone line

that kids could call. I named it the HopeLine and it started with two trained, volunteer call managers who each had a phone. At that time, I was heard on 20 stations. On the air I said, “You know, if you want to talk off-air with somebody, here is the number you can call.” The first night we received 13 phone calls. What I didn't know was how the HopeLine was going to grow and grow and grow.

In eight years, the HopeLine grew from 13 to over 18,000 calls a month. Even today, for every call the HopeLine staff handles there are still kids who can’t get their calls answered. Those kids receive busy signals or if they call outside the current HopeLine hours, they receive a recording asking them to call Monday through Thursday from 2 - 9 p.m. or Friday from 2 p.m. anytime through Monday at 6 a.m.

Some HopeLine calls are only 5 or 10 minutes long. Other times, callers need rescuing. In these cases, there are numerous contacts a staff member must make into the kids’ areas to refer them to help. Most kids in bleak situations call back five or six times. We’re glad they do. Our staff is incredibly committed to helping young people.

Now kids are telling kids who are telling more kids, “Hey, there is this HopeLine. The people really care. Call it.” Word-of-mouth is our greatest advertisement.

Because the HopeLine is not available 24 hours a day, we have purposely not marketed it beyond my radio show. As the HopeLine receives additional financial support, the number of kids who are helped will be expanded.

One Sunday night, the topic of my show was, "How has the HopeLine helped you?" A girl called and said, "I want to tell you. I became very, very depressed one winter day." She lived close to the US and Canadian border.

She continued, "I was walking to a bridge where I could jump into the icy water of the river. I got to the bridge and remembered your 800 number."

She stopped at a phone booth across the road from the bridge, called the HopeLine and the staff was there for her. She said, "If you had not come through for me, it may have been my last call."

The title of this book reflects this young woman's story which you read in Chapter One. She is one of many last calls for help that we receive.

On one hand, we are saddened that last calls exist; on the other, we are thrilled to receive last calls because we are prepared to give callers hope and turn their situations around for the better. Our heartbreak comes from wondering, "How many last calls were made to us for help when the line was busy or when we could not take those calls because we're not open around the clock?" That's why the HopeLine must be open 24 hours a day, 7 days a week and staffed to eliminate busy signals.

Imagine if we could make the HopeLine available around the clock. What if the young man in Atlanta who was feeling bad about his girlfriend breaking up with him would have made a last call before he went to the school and shot-up his schoolmates? What if? What if we here at the HopeLine could have spoken with the Columbine killers when they started to plan? What if?

We don't know "what ifs." All we know is that, right now, for every 5,000 kids we help in a month, there are 20,000 kids who can't get in. They either receive a busy signal or call when we are closed. We want to be there for students who may be making their last calls — before something really terrible happens. We want to help kids avoid the situations where they might be down to one last call.

As adults, we never know when a kid is going to need to talk. It would be nice if we could say, "Well, you know kids become deeply depressed, destructive and suicidal between 2 p.m. and 9 p.m." But it's not that simple. You never know when a teenager will be desperate enough to talk. We don't pick the time. They pick the time.

All we can do is be available and create an atmosphere that when they are ready to talk, they'll really talk. That's why it is imperative the HopeLine is expanded to 24 hours a day, 7 days a week, 365 days a year. If it's 2 a.m. and a teen needs to talk, we need to be at the other end of the phone to help.

As parents, the fact of the matter is, we don't know everything that's going through our kids' minds. We can create an environment in our homes where they will feel comfortable talking, but kids want a degree of privacy with their pain.

Most parents want to know there is a safe place for their children to turn. Even with all the concern we have for our children, there are some parents who are clueless or who just don't care. Some of the kids from those families feel alienated. They can be walking time bombs, dangerous to themselves or to others. They may act out on other kids. I believe parents who are aware of the HopeLine are thankful it is available to those kids.

We can't protect our families by building fortresses. The world is getting smaller. Needy, troubled kids, in a real sense, are affecting us all.

Just about every young person knows a kid who would pull the trigger. Young people are scared. Fear exists for adults also. We want to know how to avert these tragedies. As parents, do what you can.

Give Time And Love

Love the kids that you see. Talk to them. Watch your teenagers and their friends for signs of depression and anxiety. And give your support to the organizations that are on the front lines trying to reach these kids. It's the greatest investment you can make in saving North America.

Kids spell love as a four letter word: T-I-M-E. Who knows how much they will need — five seconds today? Five hours tomorrow? It depends on what they are struggling with. Good parents sometimes don't realize their kids are secretly dealing with issues. Single parents are in an incredible bind because they have so little time. Life is stressful and can be very difficult for them. Step families have to place their kids first. Often, when kids feel like second-class citizens, they lose hope and become angry, expressing their anger towards themselves or others. They feel insignificant and hopeless, so why should the rest of the world have any meaning or worth?

Today, my internationally syndicated call-in radio show is heard live each Sunday night on 245 stations by 500,000 listeners across North America. Graciously, each of the 245 radio stations donates the airtime as a community service for local families and especially kids who are angry and feeling hopeless.

CHAPTER 3

Opening The HopeLine 24 Hours a Day, 7 Days a Week, 365 Days a Year

Dayle Maloney

In 1997 my wife, Jeannine, and I were listening to a Sunday night program on Christian radio here in Wisconsin. The program was called *Dawson McAllister Live!* Dawson was talking to kids about their problems. He would talk to them for five or six minutes and then refer them to the HopeLine at 1-800-394-HOPE for further help.

The pain these kids were dealing with pierced our lives and our hearts. Some Sunday nights, I would have to turn the dial on the radio because my heart couldn't take listening to the rest of the call. Jeannine and I have even turned the radio down or off because we just couldn't take it. There were times I was on the road listening that I'd have to pull over to the shoulder and regain my composure.

HOW MUCH IS A LIFE WORTH?

Then Jeannine and I discovered the HopeLine was only open from 2 p.m. until 9 p.m. Even with only partial hours, over 65,000 kids are helped by the HopeLine.

We couldn't believe the HopeLine wasn't open around the clock. Jeannine and I decided the Dawson McAllister HopeLine absolutely had to be available to kids 24-hours a day, 7 days a week, 365 days a year. We call the campaign 24-7-365.

North America's teens, Jeannine and I need your help financially. We need prayers from you. We need your participation to accomplish this job for the kids. We need to see the HopeLine open 24-7-365.

What moves the people who support the HopeLine is the honesty of the kids and the magnitude of their problems. Listen to the radio show and you can hear the desperation in their voices. They are afraid their moms or dads will hear them on the show. But the kids call because they are desperate to get a chance to talk to Dawson or the HopeLine staff.

The HopeLine receives calls from kids in big cities and small towns, wealthy kids and poor kids, boys and girls. A majority of today's youth are bright, energetic and capable. They are dealing with a large volume of information that we never knew when we were their ages. We had more time to think about fewer decisions.

It's a blessing that Dawson can relate to these kids, but he can't do it alone. He needs you and me to underwrite the HopeLine so young folks can call in 24-7-365. With teenagers, we never know when they will want to talk. Sometimes it's after school while other times it's in the evening. And many times, it's at 2 a.m. or 3 a.m. when they can't sleep.

Imagine a young girl, pregnant and scared. She hasn't been able to tell anyone and is thinking about suicide. Reaching her greatest panic moment in the darkness of her parents' home at 3 a.m., she should be able to pick up the phone and dial 1-800-394-HOPE, and say "Please, help me. I have no place to turn. I'm thinking about killing myself." If we miss her call because we are not open 24-7-365, we may have missed her forever.

Each toll-free call costs the HopeLine an average of $5. We estimate next year receiving 200,000 calls. That's $1,000,000. Yes, it will cost some money to be available when North America's kids call for help. Assuredly, the HopeLine has a solid track record of turning kids' lives around for the better — even saving their lives. What if it was your son, daughter, niece or nephew and the

HopeLine was able to save his/her life? What would it be worth to you? It's worth everything if one suicide is stopped, if one girl is pulled out of a terrible sexual abuse situation or a boy is prevented from shooting up his schoolyard, killing and maiming others. If we can save one, it's worth all of what you and I can possibly do. To date the HopeLine has saved thousands.

Hundreds of thousands of young people have prayed for help. Adults like you and I are agreeing, "Okay, enough is enough. It is time to end the murders in our schools. Enough of the date rapes, the unwanted pregnancies, the sexually transmitted diseases. It's time to step in and provide support to the hundreds of thousands of teens who have prayed for it."

Get involved immediately by helping the HopeLine reach more of these kids. Take the first step now. Simply use the *"I Want To Help The Kids!"* form at the back of this book or pick up your telephone right now and call in your donation to the HopeLine office at 817-249-6000.

By supporting the HopeLine, you will be in good company. In addition to contributions from individual donors like you and me, Nutrition For Life International, a 15-year-old, publicly-traded nutritional company has stepped up with their "Gimme 5" campaign. In the following chapters we will hear from the company co-founders, David Bertrand and Jana Mitcham.

But godliness with contentment is great gain.
For we brought nothing into this world,
and it is certain we can carry nothing out.
1 Timothy 6:6,7

CHAPTER 4

THE COMPANY WITH A CAUSE

David Bertrand, President,
Nutrition For Life International

Nutrition For Life is a nutritional network marketing company whose primary objective is to make a difference in people's lives. Dawson McAllister's HopeLine has a similar mission. You and I both probably know a number of people who have needed a caring ear in a time of great need. Being able to talk over their problem and see options, where no options previously existed, made a tremendous difference in their lives. This is how Dawson and the HopeLine help people, and I believe in them.

Worldwide, Nutrition For Life makes a difference by offering parents the opportunity to earn money and time freedom from their own part-time or full-time, home-based businesses. As a company, Nutrition For Life has made a huge difference in many people's lives with our opportunity. Men and women can immediately start their own nutritional and food businesses with a very reasonable time or money investment right from their kitchen tables. People have been helped or saved with our life-enhancing products. We exist to make a positive impact in people's lives.

Nutrition For Life provides people the opportunity to achieve financial freedom but also time freedom. Our distributors can choose family over other involvements which is the greatest contribution we can make to society. I personally believe if parents had the opportunity to spend more time involved in their kids' lives, the tragic situations we see each day would never occur. Not in every case, but in many cases I believe that to be true.

I like to use the example of a woman from Canada who I met at one of our distributor meetings. She had reached the top level of her profession and earned very good money. However, one thing was missing from her life: the opportunity to participate in her two children's elementary school events. Every Tuesday, the school has Hot Dog Day. Each Tuesday morning all the parents arrive, squeeze in small chairs right next to their proud children and have hot dogs and fun. This woman was the only parent in her children's grades who had never been able to participate because of her job. Each Tuesday, her kids ate alone. She loved her job, but it was engulfing her. What she wanted out of her Nutrition For Life home-based business was to earn enough money to buy back her Tuesday mornings and have the time freedom to be with her kids.

Almost a year later, I was attending a meeting in the same Canadian city, and she shared her excitement with the people in attendance, "...because of the extra money I've made in Nutrition for Life, I've been able to take some time away from my job so that every Tuesday morning I can participate in Hot Dog Day with my two kids."

A simple decision like working from home can have an immensely positive impact on families. There is no greater act parents can perform than participating in the lives of their children.

It was through Dayle Maloney that we discovered how the Dawson McAllister Association helps young people. He began to personally support the organization and shared the results the HopeLine was having with young people. We were impressed with how they were saving and changing lives. Historically, Nutrition For Life has been very generous in our support of many causes. We've always wanted a particular cause that could represent our company and excite our 100,000 distributors.

Our challenge was to select a cause which would appeal to and directly help all our distributors. After much consideration, we selected the Dawson McAllister HopeLine as our official company cause, based on the idea that everyone wants to do something to enhance the life of a young person. I couldn't imagine anyone in our company or North America who wouldn't be in favor of helping kids.

We have made a long-term commitment to working with our distributors to create the level of support that the HopeLine deserves. We ask each of our distributors to donate at least $5 a month to the HopeLine to cover one or more calls. We call this our "Gimme 5" Campaign. The number of donating distributors is growing. It is a very easy process where monthly we debit the amount our distributors request from their accounts or credit cards and then send it to the HopeLine in the distributors' names.

Imagine the kind of blessing a $5.00 call can provide at a crisis moment in a teen's life. We never know who that young person may be. It may be someone in our family or a friend. Behind the face of every young person is a very complex story. Look deeper than the smile and we'll discover enormous stress. Who knows which kids will need a helping hand right at that critical moment? Some time in the future there could be a call from a young person who, at an extremely critical moment, needs help. Through the HopeLine a life is turned around and a productive citizen is created. It may have been your $5 that paid for the call.

***What sort of legacy will we leave?
What will they put on our tombstone?
I want mine to read that I made
a difference in somebody's life!***

CHAPTER 5

A Hero In Every Heart

Jana Mitcham,
Executive Vice-President,
Nutrition For Life International

Over the past 15 years, Nutrition For Life has received numerous requests to support various charities. Throughout the years we have been active in supporting such causes as the National Sport Wheelchair Foundation. Until now, we hadn't identified the one cause which would most powerfully represent the mission statement of Nutrition For Life: "to truly make a difference in people's lives."

When we were first exposed to the value the HopeLine provides teens, my initial thought was, "How better to make a difference in a life than when you can catch that life early?"

Who is the hope of the future but our teens? They are exposed to more temptation, more influence at a time in their lives when they want to be independent thinkers.

NUTRITION FOR LIFE CAN HELP

Nutrition For Life is a successful network marketing company which sells products that can make you healthier and wealthier. We guide our distributors to achieve their hopes and dreams. We show families how to become financially stable. The result is that people can then dream bigger.

Looking historically at the human race, people come to a point in their financial lives when they have enough to take care of themselves, and they decide to give back to society. Unfortunately, for most people that's later rather than sooner.

With Nutrition For Life's support of the HopeLine, our distributors can make a difference in the world sooner than most people. Our distributors can enjoy the dignity and self-worth of contributing without being burdened. People don't have to give thousands of dollars to support a child. Rather, we ask adults to support one call at a time, one life at a time. We think in terms of $5.00 by focusing people on the fact that for $5.00 you can support one caller. The call you sponsor could be a simple call of support or it could save someone's life.

TAKING THE BURDEN OFF PARENTS

People choose to start home-based businesses so they can be with their families. Generally, both parents are working; thus, latch-key kids are increasing. Every day, I hear how much parents want to work from home whether they are doctors, lawyers, truck drivers, retail business owners or teachers. Adults want the freedom to be home with their children. We're concerned about who is raising our children. Whose values, if any, are they using as a model? By providing kids with the HopeLine, many parents have told me, "At least while I'm away, I know there's a number my kids can call at any time."

We've also hit a generation gap where some adults don't understand their children and kids feel that parents speak a completely different language. So your child may not turn to you. If you've raised children at all, and I've raised two, you know that no matter how good the relationship, there are certain things they don't want to talk to you about for whatever reason. I've heard many of our distributors say, "I've given my kids a card with the HopeLine number and told them if anything ever comes up, keep this as an emergency number to call." What a great feeling that is. It relieves a burden of stress for parents by providing a bit of breathing time as they are developing the income which will allow them to work from home.

TEMPORARY HELP IS NOT ENOUGH FOR ON-GOING PROBLEMS

In the areas which have been devastated by school shootings, parents and schools set up temporary hotlines for teens. Why are they having to put a mechanism in place? How can they so quickly find people who are qualified to talk to teens? Where do they find the time to train the volunteers on what to say, when to speak and when not to speak? The HopeLine already exists for North American teens. It is proven and established with trained staff. As parents, let's unite and offer the HopeLine as an on-going resource to our children, 24-hours a day.

ON THE CUTTING EDGE

Corporations need to join parents in supporting causes that focus on stabilizing the family. I like the HopeLine because it shows teens how to solve their issues. Often, the HopeLine call managers will use their vast referral network to identify a helping organization in the teen's area. The HopeLine's goal is to unite families by building a bridge back to the parents. If large corporations like ours would support a cause which focuses on the family values, I think they would see employees become very excited. Their whole corporation would benefit.

ARE THE EARLY YEARS THE MOST IMPORTANT?

I was able to be with my children throughout high school. I believe if we look at what pre-teens and teens experience, we'll realize that it's a very important time for Mom or Dad to be available.

We have many distributors who, after starting their Nutrition For Life home-based business, are able to stay home. Drs. Tom and Ann Klesmit are a good example of successful professionals living a nice lifestyle who had worked outside the home. They had nannies raising their children. The Klesmits' first goal was for their home-based business' residual income to replace Dr. Ann's salary so she would be able to stay home with the kids. They achieved their goal in six months.

They have children with special challenges. The Klesmit's home-based business has given Ann the time to work with their kids and, against all odds, their children now perform at levels the experts said would never be possible.

The number one goal of Nutrition For Life is to give our distributors the choice of what they want to do with their lives. This is a home-based business where all you need is a telephone and desire, and you can be home again.

Family should always be first. Rosemary Hunt, a Canadian distributor, is a single mom whose son Kal had cancer. Being close to loved ones is important, especially when they are sick in the hospital. Rosemary has been able to be with her son every time he needed her during the past five years because she is self-employed from her home with her Nutrition For Life business.

The happiness of every family begins in the heart of a man or a woman.

CHAPTER 6

There Is More To Life Than Having Everything

David, North American Teenager

David had heard of the HopeLine on the radio while listening to the *Dawson McAllister Live!* show. The teen sporadically called the HopeLine over the course of two years about light issues. Today was much different.

David's feelings weren't showing through his poker face as he sat in the assembly room in the church basement. It was the boy's youth group night. He watched his friends run around, as mid-teens do, concerned with their newly found interest in girls and independence. While David watched his friends' hormones steam, he was boiling over himself.

Give Time And Love

"Davie boy, what's eatin' you?" His friend Mark stopped running around long enough to notice David was not at his side.

"Nothing," David replied with a blank stare.

"David, come on. Matt is telling us about makin' out with Michelle. You can't miss it!" Mark urged as he began to run towards a group of boys.

David quietly rose from his rickety folding chair and began to walk across the carpet. He approached nine young men now huddled like football players sizing up their next move. As he walked by the group, David stared straight ahead through the open side door and into the parking lot. Now was not the time to worry about kissing girls. David had much bigger issues.

His family wasn't getting along. For the last year, the stress at home had been more than he could stand. His father owned a successful restaurant and worked seven days a week. There was no time for the family. Over the past year, David had asked his father to spend time with him: ball games, church events, school happenings. His father generally said, "I'll be there," and never showed. Two days ago, when David asked his father why he wasn't at his ball game, the pressure escalated.

"David, you just don't understand, do you? I'm making a living to pay for your shoes, your clothes, your Nintendo and everything you put in your stomach. You have *everything* a kid could ask for! Where do you think the money comes from? Thin air? David, it's about time you grew up and stopped depending on me so much," his father shouted as his arms waved for emphasis. David looked towards the ground and quietly walked away.

David was sixteen. The age when he was old enough to be "the man of the house" and take out the garbage but too young to make his own decisions without checking in for his parents' permission. For days, David, the last child at home, had struggled with the feeling that he was a burden to his father. As a teen, David realized he couldn't make enough money to leave the house and live on his own. He was sure his father would love him once David stopped draining the family's bank account.

"How could God be so cruel," David thought to himself, "to give me a life, then torture me with it?" David felt trapped. He couldn't leave...where would he go? He couldn't earn money...his mother wanted him to study after school and be involved in the church youth group which met 3 times a week. David had no time to be the man his father wanted him to be.

Added to David's burden, tenth grade was harder than ninth grade. Last year none of his friends cared about girls. Now he was being called "gay" because he didn't have a girlfriend. David liked girls but wasn't ready to add a girlfriend to his stress load. He had witnessed how his friends' ex-girlfriends had devised public humiliation by starting vicious rumors or staring and laughing as an ex-boyfriend walked by in the hall. David was interested in a girlfriend but terrified of the aftermath. He tried to ignore them.

As of late, the only interaction David had with girls was when they called him "nerd", "geek" and "faggot." It wasn't so much the words. David and his friends tossed those words back and forth whenever they got together. It was the tone the girls were using. The girls would gather in a group by David's locker and quietly chant "nerd, geek, faggot" until their voices rose so loudly that you could hear their song outside in the parking lot. Then, when the volume was at full throttle, the girls would break into uncontrollable laughter. David had been taught to respect women and never raise his fist or his voice. He simply looked down at the ground and walked away. He was at the point that he didn't even want to be in school.

David was having more than his share of bad days. It seemed to David as though certain teachers could sense this and would add to his misery. David hated going to some of his classes because he felt humiliated by comments those teachers made to him. The young man's already fragile self-esteem was weakened, and he felt powerless to do anything about it.

As David sped through the open side door of the church assembly room and into the parking lot, his mind was on overload as he raced home. He was hoping if he ran fast enough, he would collapse and his heart would explode before he arrived. No such luck. Disappointment overtook him as his yard came into view.

The house was empty as he stormed in and ran up the stairs to his room. Hot, steamy tears of anger ran down his face. He couldn't stand the feelings of humiliation and worthlessness. His mind raced with only one thought. As he reached under his mattress, David felt a moment of relief as his finger was cut by a razor-sharp blade. The knife was still there. He followed the blade, cutting deeper into his finger, until he had traced his way to the handle. Grasping the knife and pulling it out into view soothed his pain despite his throbbing, bloody extremity.

He had mentally rehearsed his next move. Using his left hand to hold the knife handle, he placed the tip of the blade on the soft tissue at the base of his throat. He would use his right hand as a maul against the butt of the handle. David realized he would have one blow to plunge the knife as deeply into his throat as possible. He figured this would be a quiet death which he could execute even if his parents were home.

David sat on the floor and braced his back against the bed. With the blade at his throat, David's mind went wild, his heart raced, his breathing became sporadic. He swung his right hand as far out as he could and accidentally knocked the receiver off his phone. His eyes shot to the floor, and he momentarily listened to the dial tone.

"Call the HopeLine," a voice echoed in his mind. "David, call now."

Tears streamed down his face as his crimson finger punched 1-800-394-HOPE. He picked the receiver off the floor. With the blade still at his throat, he heard another voice.

"HopeLine, this is Brad."

David froze. There was momentary silence.

"Hey, this is Brad. Who's this?"

"David," his tone raspy as the blade pressed on his Adam's apple.

"What's up, David?" Brad asked in a curious,

yet caring manner.

"I'm going to kill myself!" David replied forcefully.

"What's going on, David. Why?" Brad asked in a calming tone.

"It's all way too much. I can't take it anymore. You can't stop me."

"David, I'm your friend and so is God. Do you think we want you to kill yourself?"

"I don't care about what you or God wants. Don't talk to me about God. He hasn't come through for me."

"I hear what you're saying, David. How has God let you down?"

"In every way."

"What about your family?"

"What about them?"

"Do you have brothers or sisters?"

"An older sister."

"Does she live at home with you?"

"No"

"Where is she?"

"She's married and lives in Kansas."

"Does she have any kids?"

"She's going to have one pretty soon."

"Her first?"

"Yeah."

"So your first niece or nephew?"

"I guess."

"Imagine your niece or nephew old enough to talk to you on the phone. Imagine that little one saying, 'Uncle David, can you come and visit me soon? When you do, can we go do something together, just us?' David, how will it feel to have your niece or nephew calling you up because he or she loves and needs you?"

David began to cry as he and Brad spoke for another 5 minutes. The knife was still at David's throat. "David, your sister and her family want you to live to be there with them. Think about them, David. Get rid of the knife; throw it across the room. Gently point it away from your throat and throw it away." Brad instructed.

David didn't want to follow Brad's guidance, but something inside of him forced his hand into action. The knife sailed across the room.

"David, where's the knife?" Brad asked.

It's sticking in my closet door," David responded in a numb, matter-of-fact tone.

"David, you made a good choice. Good job, friend. Thanks for choosing to talk to me. I care about you." Brad continued, "David, I was so concerned about you that in just a few moments you'll probably hear some people coming to your house to help you. Stay on the phone with me. They're just going to check that you're okay."

At that moment, David heard the front door open and footsteps running up the stairs.

Brad stayed on the phone with him as the police verified that David was safe. A few minutes after the police arrived, David's mother came home. She had no idea her son was contemplating suicide. It was after the police spoke to her that she realized how close to the end David had been.

Give Time And Love

David now has a support network of adults who he can turn to when pressures build. Instead of holding everything inside, he is learning to talk to safe adults. Life didn't get better overnight, but the burden of carrying the weight alone was lifted. David is developing the tools he needs to communicate with others and protect himself.

Courage is not defined by those who fought and did not fall, but by those who fought, fell and rose again.

CHAPTER 7

Teens Want Time With Parents

Tate Cockrell, Assoc. Director HopeLine & Director of Research DM Live!

Combining HopeLine experience with my degrees, a Master of Arts in Marriage and Family Therapy and a Master of Arts in Religious Education, and one year left to work on my Ph.D., I have first-hand working, knowledge of the realities of many North American families.

On an hourly basis, the call managers here at the HopeLine talk to teenagers who feel they are failing. Their relationships are the pits. Their grades are horrible. They are questioning their connection with God. Their dads or moms have just lost a job. Sometimes after I hang up the phone, I want to weep because if I had to face what these kids are dealing with I don't know how I would handle it. Just imagine Mom or Dad unemployed, desperately trying to find work. The family has no spiritual connection to lean on. The stress has the parents in constant conflict. The air is thick. Each day the parents and the kids wake up to fear and uncertainty.

A basic foundation kids need today is that both parents care and love each other. This creates comfort for children. Kids need and want to grow up in a home where they can experience safety and security. In contrast, a number of kids are afraid even in their own homes. They are afraid their parents are going to divorce, lose their jobs or not care about all or some of the family members. Many of the teens who call the HopeLine have never experienced the love and support of an all-for-one and one-for-all family. As a result of these voids, teens are acting out their anger.

With the continued teen shootings, adults and kids are becoming increasingly concerned about the anger manifesting in young adults. Most people don't realize anger is a secondary emotion which surfaces *after* someone experiences a situation resulting in disappointment, rejection or harm. People will always experience primary emotions prior to expressing anger.

A teenage boy who becomes angry with his mom and dad because they did not come to his baseball game didn't just get *angry*; he felt rejected and disappointed because his parents did not show up. His parents were not present at his game after saying they would be there for the third time. Some parents rationalize, “It doesn’t matter that I told you for the third straight time that I would be at your baseball game. Welcome to the real world. So what? You’re feeling rejected. I don’t get enough validation or appreciation, either. I don’t have anything to do with the fact that you choose to feel angry again. Get over it.” We’ve seen how teens “get over it.”

Parents must learn how to communicate and discipline — not how to punish. To discipline means to teach. How do you teach your children to be effective citizens? Most people “parent” the way they were “parented” where communication was not clear. Too many parents talk to their kids and rarely listen. A philosophy among some adults is, “Teenagers don’t have any good ideas. Every parent knows that.”

Many parents expect that they can bark a command and their teens will obey. If the teen doesn’t obey, the parents become angry or violent, inflicting punishment. In turn, the teens become angry or violent at themselves or others.

WHAT KIND OF TIME ARE WE SPENDING TOGETHER?

This is a question I posed to the participants in a parenting class which I teach at the local college. I asked for a volunteer who lived with a spouse and their children and who felt their family was typical. One man raised his hand.

"How much time do you and your wife spend together every day?"

"About 2-3 hours a night, mostly every night." he replied.

The class agreed that this couple was together more than usual.

"Is that dedicated time or time under the same roof?"

"Time where my wife and I and the kids are home at the same time."

Apparently, the kids were too young to be in school activities or gone with friends. Figuring this family was under the same roof 7 days a week, on average, this was 18 hours per week.

Next, I asked, "How much of the 18 hours are spent in conflict between you and your spouse?

He had to think about this question. After some thought and class discussion, he answered, "About 12 hours."

This means 66% of this family's time was spent fighting or trying to resolve conflict. Thirty-three percent was spent neutral or creating an atmosphere of love, joy, acceptance and support. You can't expect a child to grow up healthy in a family where conflict takes center stage. In this common situation, how could kids be expected to develop successful relationships, boundaries and communication skills? Many adults are building their children's futures on hectic schedules, financial problems, parenting skills from past generations and conflictual marriages and relationships.

UNDOING WHAT WE'VE DONE TO OUR TEENS

To increase their self-worth, kids need at least five positive communications for every negative one they receive. Let's apply this idea to the average home where 66% of all communication is negative. This means we need 330% (66% x 5) additional positive communication to neutralize the damage we inflict on our kids. That ratio is impossible. The only method to bring this ratio into check is to reduce the amount of time we adults spend in conflict with each other and our kids to 15% or less.

WHERE OUR KIDS CAN TURN WHILE WE'RE TRYING TO GET ALONG

The HopeLine and the Dawson McAllister radio show are intricately connected. One cannot exist without the other. Through the 245 radio stations which air *Dawson McAllister Live!* on Sunday nights from 7 - 9 p.m., teens discover the HopeLine is available to help them. Each week thousands of young people call into the radio show asking Dawson for personal help while over 500,000 people listen. Between Dawson's public appearances, teen conferences where he works face-to-face with kids, as well as his communication with HopeLine call managers, Dawson knows the minute-by-minute pulse of North American youth.

To keep up with the kids' needs, the HopeLine functions with a combination of staff and volunteers. HopeLine volunteers donate from 1-25 hours per week.

We are also in the process of doubling the HopeLine from 84 hours a week to 24 hours a day, 7 days a week, 365 days a year. Doing this will require more call managers who are mature Christians generally over 21-years-old. Our volunteers are very, very committed. They love kids and want to reach out with their time because of their concern for the growing apathy among North America's teen population. Our volunteers know first-hand that families are quickly disintegrating and some kids lack parental and adult role models for guidance and support. The HopeLine staff provides young people with a support system that those kids might not have otherwise. Even if we can't see them face-to-face, we can still provide the guidance and support kids need to be successful.

Success can have a rough beginning. A young lady contemplating suicide called us from a pay phone. The number had been blocked. We did not know her location. She told us her first name and that she was holding a bunch of pills in her hand. We listened to her hopelessness. Her boyfriend had broken up with her, and her family situation was grave. After much concern and listening, we asked her to make a pledge to live which we call the Contract For Life. She refused. I called our long distance company who traced the call for us, giving us the number to the phone booth. We called the police department in the area. They traced her exact location and upon arrival evaluated her as suicidal. Her parents admitted her overnight at a local hospital for a doctor's evaluation. The result could have been quite the opposite. Without the intervention of the HopeLine, she would have carried out her fatal plan.

Few parents realize when their teen is suicidal. And shockingly, many teens feel that their parents don't care if they live or die. Frequently, we receive calls from suicidal kids. We ask if they have discussed their feelings with their parents. Kids often tell us they feel that their parents don't believe them or the adults think they are faking it. Most HopeLine callers come from families where the parents aren't taking the time to figure out what's wrong. Few parents have allocated the time necessary to build trusting relationships with their kids.

Some parents think they know their kids: "My kid's not depressed," "My kid doesn't have problems," "My kid's not suicidal," "My kid's just moody." Other parents realize problems exist but refuse to admit it. When Mom and Dad admit their teen has problems, then they have to take action by looking at themselves as parents and make changes. Even adults willing to make those commitments rarely know what to do, often pretending the problem is nonexistent.

What counts is
not the number of hours you put in,
but how much you put in your hours.

CHAPTER 8

What Can Parents Expect From The HopeLine?

Kevin Coffee,
Associate HopeLine Director

The HopeLine receives many calls from suicidal students. Every one is treated very seriously. We have questions designed to assess the degree of danger the students are to themselves or others. The truth is a majority of kids really don't want to die. If we determine they are in danger and won't promise us that they won't hurt themselves, we are required by law to intervene. We have caller ID on our phones. If the phone number comes up unavailable, we contact our 800 service. Ninety-five percent of the time, they can immediately trace it for us. Often, for suicidal students or students ready to hurt others, we are their last call for help.

Give Time And Love

We offer kids a lifeline when they want it, a safe and non-judgmental haven. We don't know them, their families or their situations. This gives us the opportunity without placing blame to help students look at all their options. We have developed a strong referral base throughout North America of various services focused on helping kids. Some kids call us once; others just a few times. Yet, other kids call often. Jenny, a staff member, has had multiple phone contacts with a young caller during the course of 5 years. Jenny has become a strong source of hope, and the young lady depends on her for guidance in situations which are too embarrassing or uncomfortable to work out face-to-face with the other members of the teen's family.

Today's teens are very comfortable with long distance relationships. Over 64% of all teens are using the Internet where many develop and maintain friendships globally with people they rarely, if ever, meet face-to-face. Today's youth are accustomed to instant information, immediate response. That's why we are here and must expand to be available 24-hours a day, 7 days a week, 365 days a year.

In general, today's teens feel confused, overlooked or neglected. "No one listens to me" is a frequent comment we hear. This is why our main focus is listening to kids. There are so many distractions for parents that it becomes easier to let TV or video games keep the kids busy rather than invest quality time. Young people often relate easier to a computer, TV or Nintendo than they do to a family member. Kids aren't learning how to grow relationships during hard times. Instead, they are watching their parents hurt each other or leave. Kids are choosing safe electronic experiences over frightening family relations. This reclusive option results in a lack of social skills and confidence.

WILL STRONGER LAWS KEEP KIDS IN LINE?

Some people suggest we need to strengthen drug penalties, add more laws, put more kids in prison, and take away more guns. Does this work? We've been doing that for years and we still have growing crime rates. I think guiding moral decisions by laws misses the mark by putting a bandage on our problems, if even that. We have to start in the homes. Imagine if parents would model for their kids how to love and respect other people? How to be non-judgmental? How to accept people as they are?

At the HopeLine, we turn around the lives of kids who are gang members, prostitutes, sexually-active, drug users, rebels, loners, abused, violent and self-destructive. To use an old phrase, "We see it all." Every day, we show kids how to live happier, more fulfilled lives. We don't use laws or punishment to do this. We model relationship skills and teach them relational tools. People experience times when they have to make value judgments, but they don't have to judge the person. We show kids how to love others and accept love themselves.

Kids need to see that they can make mistakes and disappoint their parents, but their parents will still love and help them.

See to it that no one misses the grace of God.

Hebrews 12:15a

CHAPTER 9

It's Not Over 'Til It's Over

Katie, North American Teenager

Katie first called the HopeLine six years ago and continues to do so today. At that time, Katie was a typical 14-year-old Midwestern girl who was untypically pregnant by her 34-year old boyfriend. Katie was Caucasian and her boyfriend was African-American.

Upon discovering the pregnancy, her parents disowned her. Her father had a history of physically and mentally abusing Katie and her mother. He was set in his ways and would rather do away with his daughter than change his views. Because Katie's transformation was a series of phone calls over many years, she was asked to share her story:

Give Time And Love

We lived in an affluent suburb of a large Midwestern town. When my parents discovered I was pregnant, they were going to kick me out of the house. They felt I deserved to live on the streets. I wouldn't leave, even when they called the police who said my parents could get in trouble for forcing me to leave. I stayed but they refused to talk to me. They treated me like I was invisible, looking right through me. They were fighting really bad. My father would beat up my mother. He stopped beating me, probably because he was ignoring me and beating me would give me attention.

I knew my father would act that way, but I didn't know how much it would hurt me. I am the youngest of six kids. I never imagined a dad could be so mad at his child until it happened to me. It was really hard — fourteen, pregnant, still in school and my parents not there for me.

I was at a girlfriend's house when I began to slit my wrists. Just as I cut the first few layers of skin, she walked in, stopped me and promised not to tell. I figured suicide would end both my life and my baby's. That way I wouldn't feel guilty about an abortion. About a week later, I was home when I started swallowing a bunch of pills. The same friend walked into my house and to my room just as I was washing them down with water. I had the bottle in my hand. She made me puke and promised not to tell.

I wanted the pain to end so much that, I allowed the baby's father to beat me to the point where I was sure he'd kill me. I let him beat me as much as he wanted. He would do it out of anger. He got a thrill out of it. I would let him beat me to the point I couldn't walk and I passed out. My parent's didn't do anything because they had disowned me.

A girl at school noticed. I told her I was pregnant and against abortion, that I was hoping my boyfriend would beat me and my baby to death. She told me to call the HopeLine and figure out what to do. The HopeLine told me to work this through with them and things would change. They told me to stop seeing my boyfriend and gave me options besides abortion and death. The HopeLine helped me figure out if I did carry the pregnancy full term, what I would do. We decided since I was fourteen, adoption might be good. They helped me learn how to deal with my parents' lack of love and support.

I found the courage to stop seeing the baby's father. It wasn't easy but the HopeLine told me they would help with the police if he didn't leave me alone. I did have a miscarriage. The doctors couldn't tell me much about the baby because it was so deformed from the beatings.

After I started to call the HopeLine, things began to change for the better. I started to understand how to deal with my parents. They began to talk to me. The HopeLine was there for me everyday and taught me that I could make it through the hardest time of my life by going day-by-day. Things did start getting easier, and I stopped thinking about suicide. Thanks to them, I'm still here. My grades got better and I became more interested in school. I was 14 then and now I'm 20. I recently graduated from high school and have a 2-year-old daughter who is the biggest pride and joy in my life. The HopeLine helped me out. I still call them once or twice a month.

Being a parent now, I'd tell other parents to stick by their children no matter what. Help them. Don't criticize them or judge them. Be a loving parent even though it may be hard — it's harder on the child. Don't turn away from your child for any reason. It could mean life or death.

My mom thought she knew everything about me. Reality is that no parent knows everything about their kids. My mom still doesn't know everything about me. I told her about the HopeLine and how they helped me. She was very thankful. She didn't think anybody would take the time and energy to sit down and listen to teens.

If parents think, "My kids don't need the HopeLine. They're not hurting that much," they're wrong. Most parents don't realize how bad their kids are hurting. If parents haven't built strong relationships through the years, and when kids become teens, they trust their friends more than the parents who didn't spend time with them. My parents told me they thought they gave me enough time. Whenever we did talk, what I said would go in one ear and out the other, or they would spend our time together judging me and telling me why I was wrong.

I want kids to realize when they can't confide in their parents, they should confide in a friend that might be able to help them. I found my way out because a friend gave me the HopeLine number. After I talked with the HopeLine, I could confide in my parents.

Even though my mother was thankful for the HopeLine, I think it hurt her that we didn't have the kind of relationship she thought we did. It was at that point, when she changed and started to become a mom to me. Hopefully, other parents will realize they have to stop judging and punishing and start talking and guiding their children.

PART 3

Teenagers Are Crying Out

CHAPTER 10

Are Kids Struggling More Today?

Dawson McAllister

In my book, *Saving The Millennial Generation*, I cite *Group*, a magazine about youth ministry, who asked several experts to share their views on what today's kids are facing compared to kids twenty years ago (which is roughly one generation). Here are their observations:

George Gallup (Co-chair of the Gallup Organization)

The past 20 years have brought more of humanity's blessings and burdens into the minds and onto the shoulders of teenagers. An explosion of communications technology left few of the world's secrets untold, and, as usual, young people learned faster than their elders.

A few television networks have given way to hundreds of channels that soon may number thousands. Almost any kind of information can be received any time and anywhere. Through satellite communications, today's teen may know more about events in Bosnia than in Boston. Millions of young people soar through cyberspace to exchange experiences on personal computers. The pace cars of the information superhighway are driven by teenagers. As a result, there are few local fads in the teenage global village.

It is no doubt impossible to judge the total impact of the communications revolution on teenagers. What is certain, however, is that it has brought them more fully into the global society and given them a larger share of the perils and pleasures of their time.

Wayne Rice (Co-founder of Youth Specialties)

Today's kids don't have the support systems that were in place 20 years ago. The loss of the two-parent nuclear family and the extended family has had enormous impact on the well-being and healthy development of kids. They are more alone, more dependant on their peers, have a more difficult time making decisions and answering questions of identity and purpose. That's one reason why the best youth workers are very relational, very family-oriented.

Martin Marty (Author, Speaker, Professor of Modern Christianity at the University of Chicago)

The biggest impact is the flow and flood of impulses from all directions — peers, school, TV and advertising. These have always been there, but the difference between 20 years ago and now is that there are fewer filters, fewer fortifications. There's less intactness to the family, to the clubs, to the after-school activities in high school, to the church youth group, to the neighborhood — to all these elements that used to make it possible for parents to help screen the worst from the adolescent. There are fewer instruments that would help teens interpret what's coming their way.

Neil Howe (Expert Futurist and Co-author of *The Fourth Turning*)

I would say probably the biggest shift in the last two decades would be worries about upward economic mobility. In the 70's, young people's expectations were still unbelievably optimistic about their future. Now, everybody talks about money — even in junior high.

Households under age 30 have lost about 15 percent in household income due to inflation in the last 20 years. There has been an enormous divergence in the economic fortunes of older and younger Americans. The last several years have been difficult for graduating seniors. A lot of people realized they'd played by the rules — went to college, got the degrees and worked hard. But there was just nothing out there for them. They ended up driving a UPS truck. That's sobering, and I think that reality has filtered down to high school.

George Barna (Founder and President of Barna Research Group)

Among the most critical changes in the last 20 years:

1. The dramatic increase in the number of lifestyle choices available to kids.
2. The reduction in the number and understanding of moral and ethical absolutes and limitations.
3. The quickening of response time in decision-making, resulting in spontaneous decisions based on minimal reflection.

4. The substantial surge in the volume of information available —quite conveniently and inexpensively — on a vast array of topics.
5. The lower personal standards to the heightened level of expectations we have of other people and institutions.
6. The increase in stress and anxiety, along with the decrease in hope and joy.
7. The deterioration of the family as a stable base of support.
8. The demise of other social institutions focused upon providing support for young people.
9. An exceedingly intrusive opinionated media which passes along its own biases as objective reporting.

Life can only be understood
by looking backward,
but it must be lived
by looking forward.

CHAPTER 11

The Evolution Of Teens

Dawson McAllister

In his book, *The Rise And Fall Of The American Teenager*, Thomas Hines points out that the term "teenager" itself is young. It dates from the 1940's when it described a new consumer market.

Since that point, each new generation finds teenagers facing the same basic struggles to find their identity, purpose, independence, and direction in life. What changes through the years are the circumstances. Are we dealing with borrowing the reins to the horse or the keys to the car? Will kids see sex for the first time between chickens on the family farm or will they be alone in their room when they press a button on their computer and instantly be witness to illicite sex?

Teenagers Are Crying Out

What previous generations learned in their twenties, many kids today are having to deal with as pre-teens. Information is forcing our kids to grow up faster, before they have developed the skills to deal with the pressures of adulthood.

Pollster and social analyst George Barna explains the challenge facing today's kids: typically, they are required to make decisions quicker than ever before, yet they spend little time with adults who might provide wisdom and direction.

Kids have become accustomed to rapid-fire media images, instant access to the Internet, fast food and speed in almost every area of their lives. They have an incredibly vast array of knowledge available to them 24-hours a day on the Web and they use it. Decision making has become almost spontaneous. In addition, the average teen today spends twelve *fewer* hours per week relating to his/her parents than did the average teen in 1980. This combination provides plenty of information, but very little wisdom.

There was a time when children grew directly to adulthood. Most of their childhood was spent working alongside their parents, siblings and extended family in shops or on farms. There was plenty of time to think, reflect, consider and ask questions of adults. The kids gathered their information from the adults around them.

Farm life found families living and working together 24 hours a day, 7 days a week. Each person contributed to the welfare of all. Children gathered eggs for breakfast. If they didn't, someone else would have to neglect his or her work to collect eggs. As simple as this job sounds, uncollected eggs would rot and the family would lose valuable food. Children's contributions were important. On a daily basis, kids could feel the satisfaction of their accomplishments towards the good of the family.

The industrial revolution changed people's lives as large, extended families scattered from farms to live as immediate families in the cities where separation occurred. Time together was left to the hours after work. Most people worked 12 hours a day, six or seven days a week. Since children were either working or left to fend for themselves while their parents were at work, diversions were created such as games, books, church and later radio.

In the 1960's the technological revolution began to take shape. Suddenly computers, televisions and electronics of all kinds promised to make life easier and more entertaining. For the first time, family members turned their attention from each other to the television. A significant amount of time, which family members previously spent talking to each other, was replaced with simply sitting in the same room listening to the person on the tube. The amount of information being pumped into the home about the outside world was increasing. The amount of time spent as a family unit listening to parental guidance was decreasing.

Next came the information explosion of the 1980's when computers invaded homes in large numbers and people began to hook up to the Internet. Of course, it was young people who were more interested in the new "fad" than oldsters. This meant young people were adding to their information overload long before older people. Suddenly, these teens had access to new information — more than most anyone dreamed possible — including forbidden topics. If parents chose not to talk to their teens about sex, drugs and feelings, the people with Web pages would. The Internet continues to be a vast space for free speech where people can advertise or say absolutely anything they want.

I'm not against technology; rather, I want to show how we have come to this point in our society's history. While we can remember a time before technology, our children can't. Today's teens take technologies for granted. They grew up immersed in it. The Internet and today's kids equal astronomical growth. More than ten million children have accessed the Internet in the past year. The figure is double from the previous year, which was double from the year before.

One teenage girl described why she and her friends are flocking to the Internet: "I can get on-line and talk to my friends more personally, privately and safely than if I were face-to-face. People can't see any of my flaws like if I'm overweight, have acne or I'm too shy to speak to their faces. The Internet is great because it forces us to write and use our English skills. I can leave messages for friends after it's too late to call them on the phone. I can talk to them when I want, and they can answer me when it works for them."

Teens can pull up more than one million Web sites on every imaginable topic: philosophies, sex, drugs, writing, sports, news, and many others. Without an adult's opinion, kids may view these topics as equal options. Chat lines are also exciting to kids. They can say anything they want without having to talk face-to-face. Most of the time this is harmless fun, but on some occasions danger can be present.

A 15-year-old girl called the HopeLine after she met a new boyfriend over the Internet. He was 53-years-old and had just sent her an airline ticket to visit him for the weekend. The anticipation of his promises. . . flying in an airplane, driving his car and shopping all weekend. . . was exciting to her. She had devised a plan to cover for her absence from home and was calling us because she was getting last minute jitters. Some friends told her to go: "It'll be fun." Others asked her why she wanted to spend the weekend with "some ancient guy." After a lengthy conversation with the teen, she began to understand the potential danger. The young lady volunteered the man's name, location and where they were going to meet in the airport. The police were called, and in turn, met the 53-year-old suitor at the airport gate.

Healthy development requires considerable interaction between children and their parents, siblings and peers. When this development is stifled, we all suffer. Too often the fascination of computer games and software draws a teen into the world of the "square-headed friend." To understand our kids better, we need to understand computers. We need to "walk a mile in our kids' shoes," which today could be translated into "surf the Web an hour or so."

CHAPTER 12

Who's Loving Our Kids?

Dawson McAllister

According to a 1997 report by the *Journal Of The American Medical Association*, "approximately 17% of 12 and 13-year-olds and 49% of 14 through 18-year-olds indicated they have had sexual intercourse."

Safe sex or not, Dr. Joe McIlhaney, Jr. of the Medical Institute for Sexual Health reports that condoms fail to block HIV 31% of the time. Each year, approximately 3,000,000 American teenagers acquire a STD (sexually transmitted disease). Adolescents (10-19 years of age) are at the greatest risk for acquiring a STD because they are more likely to have multiple sex partners and engage in unprotected intercourse. Female adolescents are more susceptible to cervical infections such as gonorrhea and chlamydia because the cervix is especially sensitive to infection in young women.

The high divorce rates of the past twenty years and the increase in teen sex may have a strong parallel. As fathers have been absent from the home environment, or almost absent because they choose to work seventy or eight hours a week, they obviously have less time to spend nurturing and directing their children. With the rapid rise of both parents working, children in these families are often left with a great need for warmth, love and positive attention. On average, parents and teens personally interact 14 minutes a day, 12 minutes of which is negative.

Teenagers, especially girls, mistake sex for intimacy. In a survey by *Seventeen* magazine, only 1.1% of girls said sex was more important to them than love and affection. Yet, sadly, 12 to 19-year-old girls who are longing for affectionate, loving relationships are often settling for sex.

The *Journal Of The American Medical Association* reported that pledges of abstinence, religion, high expectations in school and strong, loving, accepting families all play a significant role in delaying the onset of sexual activity.

DEALING WITH VIOLENCE

A study conducted by the Recreational Software Advisory Council of Cambridge, Massachusetts, found 46% of computer games contained violence and 48% of them received a Violence #2 rating or above which is equivalent to an R movie. This means humans are being killed or injured with all the blood and gore associated with it.

Violence is not the only concern with video games. Several years ago, a University of Miami study of top-rated computer games revealed that almost 90% excluded women from any leading roles. Male figures dominated by a 13 to 1 ratio. Perhaps worse, in the plots of almost 33% of the games, women were depicted as helpless victims who needed to be rescued by men.

Recently, we spoke to a youth pastor who told us one of the teens in his youth group was spending $250 a month on computer games. When the youth pastor asked the young man about it, the teen replied, "When I play computer games, the people on the other side can't really hurt me. I'm safe playing these games."

Teens are being hurt in two ways. Number one, they are fixating on a relationship with a video game rather than relationships with humans where the kids would develop emotionally. Number two, kids believe the lie that violence has no consequences. Shoot the guy on the screen, turn off the computer and walk away when you're done.

I believe the recent killings in high schools are, in part, the result of kids believing violence is normal and sanitary. The blood and gore in the video games are cleaned up with the push of a computer button. Could the kids who have killed thought the victims would get up and go on with life when the "game was over"? Did they realize the blood and funerals were real? Did they think that somehow they would press a button on their computer keyboard and everything would start over and be okay?

The pervasive violence in movies, television and especially interactive computer video games has a numbing effect. Kids are led to believe they can shoot people, turn off the screen and go out for pizza. Their minds and perceptions have been terribly wounded.

BOMBS

For years we have heard of people finding the designs for bombs on the Internet. People old enough to type the word "bomb" into an Internet search engine are shown detailed plans to make almost any type of incendiary device imaginable, from simple pipe bombs (such as the one used at the Atlanta Olympic Games) to nuclear devices.

SMUT

Parents are understandably outraged about the ease with which their children can access pornography. And it seems to be everywhere! For instance, in completing research for this book the word "teenager" was entered into a popular search engine. The search revealed tens of thousands of sites. The researcher began to scroll through headlines matching our search word and found herself in the middle of scores of listings of teen pornography with the most graphic descriptions ever seen. The Internet is rampant with pornography.

In 1998, the HopeLine fielded 65,000 calls; 1,500 were from young people addicted to pornography. Since pornography is a secretive problem, I would guess the number of people affected is greater than this figure suggests.

A short time ago, the Mars space mission drew the attention of millions of people. When many of them tried to access NASA, they typed in the Web site address of NASA.com instead of the official address of NASA.gov, which contained the up-to-date information about the mission to Mars. When school children made this common mistake, they were taken to a hardcore pornography site complete with detailed pictures.

DECISION MAKING

Technology is setting the pace for our lives. Instant gratification is the way we choose to live. Advertising and competition make users, young and old, dissatisfied and impatient with anything but the latest, greatest and fastest on the market. We have little time for reflection but are forced to make quicker decisions. Adults and children are spending fewer hours together which means kids have less access to wisdom when they are under peer pressure to make quicker decisions.

SELF-MUTILATION

One of the rages among adolescents today is body piercing. Walk in the mall for a few minutes (it won't take long, I assure you) and you'll see kids with every part of their bodies tattooed or pierced. Ears? That's old-fashioned unless you have a dozen or more rings on all parts of your ears. More trendy piercing includes eyelids, noses, tongues and belly buttons. Genital piercings are now popular, too. In states where you have to be 18 or have parental consent to have your body pierced, kids are piercing their own and their friends' body parts.

And tattoos aren't just for motorcycle riders anymore. Many girls are tattooing their ankles, shoulders, breasts, butts and inner thighs. Of course, guys are getting their arms done. For most teens, body piercing or tattooing today is not much different from long hair and ducktails in the 1960's.

The more alarming aspect of this trend is self-mutilation. Psychologist Lynn Ponton, author of *The Romance of Risk: Why Teenagers Do The Things They Do*, believes that kids today are bored, so they burn, cut and disfigure themselves as a form of exhilarating achievement. Ponton states, "There is less for teens to do today in risk-taking, so they're turning to their own bodies."

For some, the goal is an outlandish new body form such as inserting objects under the skin to form knobby growths on the head or forehead that become horns, or taking out ribs so the waist can be 15 inches. But for others the pain involved is the goal itself. An article in the *San Francisco Chronicle* described one girl, Amy, who has scarred hands from digging her fingernails into them for years. She also broke windows in her mother's house in order to cut herself. "I like pain," she said flatly. "Pain is like a drug. It can be either a good or bad drug. It can either enhance or destroy."

The cult of pain in San Francisco welcomed Amy and her friend, Ivy, who remembered, "When I found there was an actual scene here, it made me feel that I was okay. I wasn't a freak." The group asked her to use a cattle iron to brand herself on stage at a club. She agreed.

Ivy reminisced, "It was like going to another level. How much can I take? It's like being in another state of mind." Ivy was branded on her upper arm in four sections, searing her skin each time. "I liked it. I liked the smell. That was part of it." Several months later, when the branding marks began to fade, Ivy was branded again.

Like Amy and Ivy, an estimated 2,000,000 adolescents in North America are self-mutilators. The writer for the *Chronicle* stated, "Psychologists say that cutting and other self-injury provides temporary relief from intense feelings of anxiety, anger or depression — a theory that seems to be supported by science. Cutting the skin releases beta-endorphins, the body's natural pain-killer. The endorphins can actually boost one's mood. Indeed, many who return repeatedly to the piercing shops describe an elation during and after the pain. Over a period of time, a person usually must inflict more frequent and more acute pain in order to achieve the same sensation."

Dr. Armando Favazza, professor of psychiatry at the University of Missouri Medical School calls this practice "a morbid form of self-help."

DESPERATE FOR LOVE

I see thousands of teenagers who desperately want to be loved, who feel so lonely that they can't stand it any longer. I received this letter after one of my conferences:

Dear Dawson,

I need to be loved. I've prayed to God that I could have assurance and I still feel alone. Family is important? How so when you become the shadow in your own house. Relationships are to fulfill the other part of you. I am supposed to have a significant other. I'm sorry but I have been ready to die for love for the past few weeks. A hug could do wonders, but 5 minutes later I feel lonely again. No one has said, "Sandra, I love you" and meant it fully in the past 2 or 3 weeks. I want help, yes. But I am stuck in my ways. I despise change. I need you to tell me how to make my mother and sister love me again.

You're my last hope,
Sandra

Teenagers Are Crying Out

Kids communicate their sense of abandonment in many ways. I received this beautiful and haunting poem from a lonely young person:

No one sees
Me fall to my knees
I drop to the floor
I cannot run anymore
I've run for so long
So many things have gone wrong
I don't know how, I don't know why
All I know is I want to die
Oh, God! What should I do
I want to begin life anew
Without any enemies, problems or depression
My problems have become my obsession
No one hears
My bittersweet tears
No one cares
No one dares
No one knows
I guess that's the way it goes
Every day
I try a new way
To lose my sadness
I haven't a clue
Of what I should do

One night on my radio program, I received a call from a girl who was in pain. She told me, "Well, my parents, they've been like going through this divorce for a long time. They got separated like two years ago and then they got back together but...my dad, he. . .like. . .would like beat me and stuff."

I asked, "A lot?"

"Yeah, My mom used to work nights or at the second shift so she would be gone from when I got home from school until I would...after I would go to bed, and my dad, he'd come home and freak out and take out all of his anger on me and my sister every night almost."

"So you were getting beaten almost every night?"

"Yeah," she said softly.

"How old were you at the time?"

"Well, it, um, almost all my life up until two years ago, until I was twelve."

At 14-years-old, Susan had bottled up her hurt and anger. As she and I continued to talk, she said, "I'm afraid if I started really crying, it will just all gush everywhere...I'm terrified for that to happen. I might never stop."

We continued to talk and Susan shared her deep hurts with the radio audience. I told her about experiencing God's forgiveness so she could forgive her father for hurting her. Susan also needed to forgive her mother for not protecting her from her dad. I assured her that those who were listening would be praying for her. Then, I directed her to call the HopeLine for additional help.

Millions of young people feel disconnected from, or worse, battered by family and friends. Unfortunately, they believe they have nowhere to turn.

The night is far spent,
the day is at hand:
let us therefore cast off
the works of darkness,
and let us put on
the armour of light.

Romans 13:12

CHAPTER 13

High School Horror

Julie, North American Teenager

Julie was listening to *Dawson McAllister Live!* She heard Dawson talk about kids calling the HopeLine at 1-800-394-HOPE. Without hesitation, she dialed the phone.

"HopeLine, this is Judy, " expecting to reach the radio station, Julie was shocked and hung up the phone.

Sitting in the dark of her bedroom, Julie picked up the phone and called the number again.

"HopeLine, this is Kirk." Hearing his voice, Julie took a deep breath.

"Ahh, hi." Julie managed to squeak out.

"Hi, this is Kirk. Who is this?"

She paused and then said quietly, "Julie."

"Hey, Julie. How you doing tonight?"

"Oh, I'm okay." Julie said half-heartedly.

"What would you like to talk about?"

"Well, not much really."

"Okay. You lead. I'll listen."

"Well, I'm not doing so good."

"Sounds like you might be feeling some pain, Julie. What's it about?"

"Ahh, I snuck out of the house Friday night and things got really bad."

"How so?"

"Well, this guy he..." Julie choked as tears overtook her.

"It's hard, Julie. Take your time and tell me about this guy."

Julie paused. She couldn't bear to say anymore. She wanted to hang up but felt that Kirk was there for her, that he really cared. The silence was too long so Julie broke, "He. . . he raped me."

"Are you okay, Julie? Are you safe now?"

"Yes, I'm safe but I'm not feeling okay. I can't stand the idea of going to school tomorrow and seeing him. I just want to kill myself. I can't tell my parents because I snuck out of the house when they told me to stay home. It's a big mess and it hurts a lot. I just want to end it all." Julie cried in a piercing tone.

"Julie, I believe you about the pain and your desire to end it all, but I want you to live. It doesn't feel like it now, but life is worth living. Together, you and I, we can deal with this situation and make it better for you. Can you promise me that you won't hurt yourself?"

"No, I can't promise anything. Are you kidding? I was raped by this guy I know from school while everyone else watched. How can I ever live that down? After it was done, people said it was my fault. They made fun of me. They called me a slut and said that I wanted it." Julie was out of breath from the tears, pain and embarrassment.

"Julie, if I promise to make this right for you, will you promise to not hurt yourself? Julie, you've already been hurt enough. I'll bring your pain to an end and you'll still be here on earth. You know, Julie, you have a purpose in your life to fulfill. You were sent here to help a lot of people. You can only help those people if you choose to live. Julie, promise me that you'll choose to live. What happened to you was wrong and not your fault. It was everyone else's fault who watched without protecting you. It was the fault of the boy who raped you. Julie, I believe you. Will you make me the promise that you won't hurt yourself?"

"I can't go to school on Monday."

"Julie, you don't have to go to school on Monday."

"I don't want to tell my parents."

"Do you feel that your parents love you?"

"Yes."

"Would they want to protect you and help you?"

"Probably."

Julie and Kirk talked for another 5 minutes. Though Julie eventually said she would not hurt herself, Kirk could hear she was becoming more and more desperate. Before Julie hung up, the HopeLine had traced her call and the local police were on their way to her house.

As Julie laid on the floor looking through tears at the bottle of pills in her hand, she was jolted from her pain by a loud bang against her locked bedroom door. She threw the pills under her bed, rose in the darkness and opened her door. She was blinded as a police officer pointed his flashlight into her eyes. Her mother followed the police into Julie's room and turned on the light.

"What's going on?" Julie rubbed her eyes implying this was some kind of mistake.

"Are you Julie?"

"Yeah"

"We received a call from the HopeLine that you were thinking about hurting yourself."

"I don't know what you're talking about."

One of the officers picked up the phone and pushed "redial."

"HopeLine, this is Kim."

"This is Officer Stanley. Would you please put Kirk on the phone?"

The other officer began to question Julie as her father entered the room.

"It wasn't me. You have the wrong house, the wrong person. I don't know what you're talking about," Julie pleaded as she looked towards her parents who were standing over the officer's shoulder. Julie became increasingly angry as she thought to herself, "How could they have narked on me? I hate the HopeLine."

Kirk was on the phone and could hear Julie's voice arguing with the other officer. "That's her voice." He reassured the officers they had the right person. Kirk asked officer Stanley to take Julie to the side without her folks and privately talk to her about the rape. "Please, she is really scared about telling her parents. That, and facing this kid and her friends tomorrow is why she wants to kill herself. I'm sure she's really mad at me right now and won't talk to me. Help her tell her family and keep her dignity."

The officer assured Kirk that he would handle Julie's situation with care and respect.

"Julie, Kirk identified your voice. We know you made the call."

Julie's shoulders dropped as she silently looked towards the floor.

Officer Stanley looked at Julie's parents. "Could we have a word alone with Julie, for just a moment. We just want to help her and sometimes kids find it easier to talk without parents in the room."

They agreed to step into the hallway.

"Julie, I know about the rape two nights ago. Kirk knows and said you haven't told your parents. Who is helping you with this?"

"My youth counselor at church." Julie lied hoping that answer would be enough to get the police to leave.

"When do you plan on telling your parents?'

Julie remained silent.

"Julie, you're a minor and they have to know. Besides, they love you and would want to know. Why don't we tell them together?"

"No, I don't want them to know."

"Julie, if you've told your youth minister, your parents are going to find out anyway. He has to report rape. This boy raped you and if you don't tell your parents, he'll possibly rape another. Julie, do you want another girl to go through what you did?"

Julie's mind instantly flashed back to the helpless moments as her 105-pound body was overtaken by a 250-pound football player who was laughing, while choking and violating her. She opened her tear-filled eyes and said angrily, "No, I don't want anyone to go through that!"

"You're right, Julie. What he did was wrong and we have to put an end to it. That end starts with letting your parents help you. Do you want to tell them, or should we do it together?"

"I'll tell them."

The officer stood next to Julie while she told her parents what happened. Julie's mother buried her face in her hands, overtaken with grief and anger. Julie's father wanted to know the boy's name so he could even the score. The officer recommended a better way of dealing with the boy: press charges.

Julie's family was highly involved in the local church and immediately set up a support network for her. She worked with a youth pastor and a support group for other young people who had been sexually violated.

Within a week, Julie called the HopeLine and thanked Kirk. He told her, "I'm here for you, and so is everyone else here at the HopeLine."

Julie knew that was true.

Two weeks after the event, Julie returned to school. It was *not* a warm reception. The rapist was the school's star football player. He was kicked off the team in the middle of play-offs. Her school was in the running for its first state title in over 10 years. The team had lost two games and state title hopes without its star player. The kids blamed Julie and even though students witnessed the rape, many said Julie was lying. Cruel rumors were spreading and the tension was grueling. Julie lost her desire to graduate. Arrangements were made for Julie to complete a majority of her senior year schoolwork from home.

About a month after the rape, Julie was devastated again when it was discovered that she was pregnant. She and her family had to deal with a new set of issues. From the stress of reliving her rape during the court appearances or just because it wasn't meant to be, Julie had a miscarriage.

The young man was sentenced as an adult and served 90-days.

Amazingly, Julie graduated from high-school. "I probably would not have been here or stayed in school without the HopeLine. The guy I talked to had a different way of getting his point across. Now I know that I can call the HopeLine for help anytime I need it."

Julie continued, "I know how to deal with it now and have gone to counseling. The main thing that happens is every now and then I have nightmares. I get up and write in my journal. Before the rape I was really on fire about life. Everything was great. After the rape I went into depression."

Julie took the summer to "just be a kid." The fall will find her in Bible college. "I'm just following my heart, one day at a time."

Be strong and of good courage,
fear not, nor be afraid of them;
for the Lord thy God;
He it is that doth go with thee;
He will not fail thee; nor forsake thee.

Deuteronomy 31:6

CHAPTER 14

Dealing With Shame

Traci,
HopeLine Call Manager

Last night, I received a call which was most touching for me. A girl called saying that her father was a youth minister. She wanted to know what she could do to get her father to spend as much time with her as he did with the church youth. I thought this was a pretty profound statement. I know of ministers who neglect their families in favor of their congregation. I think that's wrong. She told me, "I hate the fact my father's a minister."

We talked about her feelings. About 20 minutes into the conversation, I discovered that she was raped about a month ago and was pregnant. Her father didn't know. She said, "I just hate what this is going to do. It's going to destroy him."

I asked, "Is that why you hate that he's a minister?"

She answered, "Yeah."

My heart ached because she felt the rape was her fault. She knew the man, and it was date rape. She felt if she hadn't gone on the date, the rape could have been prevented. The teenager felt real dirty and was dreading telling her father. From her description of her father, he seemed like a very loving, Godly man. Any good father is going to help his child.

The measure of people is not how great their faith is but how great their love is.

CHAPTER 15

Taking The Time To Listen

Lori,
HopeLine Call Manager

Today, many kids face a great deal of pressure to grow-up quickly or have to make decisions that are not meant for kids their age. Last week, a *10-year-old* called about the pressure she was feeling to have sex with a certain boy. She didn't know what to do.

I received a call from a boy saying, "I went to my school counselor about this problem, but she didn't take me seriously. I need somebody to take my problem seriously."

Here at the HopeLine, we take each call seriously. We listen and link the kids up with the ongoing support they need. That may be bridging them back to their parents, locating affordable, professional help in their area, being here for calls as they need or some combination.

What I hear most often from kids is that they want more encouragement and positive time with their parents. They want their problems respected and taken seriously. Kids hate to hear from their parents, “You think you’ve got problems? Wait until you get to be an adult. Why don't you try living in my shoes?” That's really negative. It’s the quickest way to stifle kids, and as we’ve seen in the news, that can be dangerous.

And, ye fathers,
provoke not your children to wrath:
but bring them up in the
nurture and admonition of the Lord.

Esphesians 6:4

CHAPTER 16

Volunteering For The Kids

Ronnie,
HopeLine Call Manager

I volunteer every Sunday night to answer phone calls from kids who call into the HopeLine. Because of Dawson's radio show, this is the time when we have our highest call volume.

I received a call from a 20-year-old guy who had called a couple of weeks earlier about his finance who was dying of leukemia. She had passed away and he was devastated, his words cutting in and out through his tears. He had been in his room since the funeral Saturday morning. From our previous conversation, I knew he had a spiritual background, so for an hour I read scriptures, consoled him and listened.

At one point I said, "You know, I feel like I need to pray for you." We stopped and prayed together. After our prayer he told me that his girlfriend had left him a letter — he hadn't been able to open it. I asked if he would like to read it together. He did. She told him that she wanted him to go on with his life. She knew he would be grieving for a while, but he had his own life to live. She wanted him to go on. At that point, he felt a moment of peace and comfort; then he became overwhelmed again.

I tried to refocus him by asking, "What are you going to do tomorrow?" He hadn't thought about it, saying, "I don't know." We developed a plan to do a little bit, just to get him out of his bedroom. He agreed to leave the house for an hour or more for lunch with a friend and then to visit a bookstore for material on grieving. He also promised that after our call he'd fix himself something to eat as he hadn't eaten in two days. He had plenty of food but no appetite. He agreed to give me a follow up call.

CHAPTER 17

Showing Kids the Light

Larry Bone, Executive Director
Dawson McAllister Association

Kids call the HopeLine and the radio show with all kinds of issues.

Some are simpler issues: I can't make friends; People are picking on me; I just moved and don't know anyone.

Some are middle of the road: I just had a fight with my mom or dad; I just broke up with my boyfriend or girlfriend; I got dumped.

Then, we get into heavier issues: My parents are divorcing and I think it is my fault; I've been sexually abused by a friend, a neighbor, a relative, my father; I'm suicidal; I'm anorexic; I'm using drugs; I want to kill or hurt other people because they hurt me.

In their eyes, all questions can be life and death issues. Kids can feel hopeless over very small issues because they see no way out. Their circumstances are really not hopeless. Rather, some situations might be almost laughable to adults, but to kids they can be deadly serious. Here at the HopeLine, we help young people who may not have the ability to see the bright side or all their options.

The value of wisdom is far above rubies; nothing can be compared with it.

Proverbs 8:11

PART 4

Pain Relief For Your Soul

CHAPTER 18

When Teens Talk, We Listen

Dawson McAllister

When I began working with kids in June of 1968, as a society, we had far more structure to our lives. We had greater trust for authority figures and institutions — the church, government, parents, schools. Families were far more in tact than today. We didn't know about AIDS or MTV.

The changes which occurred in the 1970's and 1980's were gradual. Teenagers began swimming upstream and in the early 80's it was obvious they were struggling. With the gradual changes in the way we lived and the growing infrequency of family communications, teenagers wrestled with unfulfilled needs.

In 1975, which was seven years into my teenage

ministry, I noticed the change in teens. A youth leader and I held a spiritual youth conference on Catalina Island, California with no reason to expect this conference to be any different than the hundreds of others I had attended. A large number of kids signed up indicating they wanted further spiritual help. The agenda was based on a series of pre-conference meetings where kids were asked what they wanted to learn. The kids said they wanted to know how to pray, read the Bible, know God and be forgiven.

But shortly after the conference started, the kids experienced a real drop-off in interest. One of the kids said, "You know, I care about these things but I can't get along with my parents." Another privately told me, "This stuff is good, but, I'm sleeping with my boyfriend. I think I'm pregnant."

During that conference, I was shocked to hear so many of the teenagers talk about their unhappiness at home or their desire to run away. The conference took a sudden turn from studying the Bible to talking about the real, day-to-day issues those teenagers were facing. I called these issues "felt needs."

I became aware that kids needed help with these problems before they would even consider listening to spiritual issues. So as a result, I focused on meeting teens' needs first.

I wrote *Discussion Manual for Student Relationships* which was used by youth leaders throughout North American to help teens accept themselves, get along with their parents, deal with loneliness, face temptation, etc. I became keenly aware that kids were asking very practical, personal "felt need" questions. I discovered when these issues were addressed in honest and practical ways, kids would listen.

I live by the old adage, "If you want to go out and talk to somebody about God, but they are starving to death, there is a good chance they're not going to hear what you have to say about God until you feed them." The teens I worked with had been hurt. Their trust had gone out the window and had been replaced by self-blame, self-hate and either anger or depression. Until I helped them overcome their pain, the kids rejected talk about morals, values or right and wrong.

Many experts agree and my experience reveals that kids who are in pain and highly frustrated have distrust towards authority figures. Why? In many situations, abusers have a degree of mental or physical power over their child victims. The children view their perpetrators as authority figures. Prior to the disappointment or abuse, the young people usually trust these authority figures. The abusers use this trust against the children. The result? Kids blame themselves for trusting and vow not to make the same mistake again.

How often has this cycle repeated itself? Fifty percent of the 30,000,000 teenagers or 15,000,000 kids have been sexually abused, only one of many forms of abuse or disappointment with which our children are dealing. Couple this figure with the volume of kids experiencing other abuses and disappointments...and we have created a generational distrust of authority.

But, they'll grow out of it, right? They'll learn to trust?

It's not *whether* they'll trust but *who* they will trust.

In the late 1960's, teens were far more socially-oriented towards large groups. They were much more open to discussing the issues of their lives and how to cope. In comparison, today many kids are far more isolated. Although they receive more information, they feel much safer interacting with a computer screen versus other humans.

A generation ago, kids ran away to someone. Today, rather than running away, they are mentally pulling away. In some cases, they are withdrawing into their own minds and peer groups who mirror their feelings. A number of teens have moved into small, niche groups. "The Trenchcoat Mafia" of

Columbine High School is an example of one such group. In these groups, kids find comfort from other people who think similarly.

Here's an example of the difference between generations. Think about the movie *Grease*. Some of the guys wore leather coats. Some wore cloth. Some of the young women wore dresses. Others wore pants. Each person had his or her own thoughts and beliefs that were different from the other people in the group. Danny was a jock who liked sports. Kenickie liked to wrench on cars and wasn't impressed by sports. Danny wanted to look good. Kenickie fought and often his desires were questioned by his peers. Yet, the teens accepted each other's differences.

Today, the groups tend to be much more niched. If a kid likes sports, s/he is more likely to hang around with other kids who participate in sports. If a kid often feels angry, s/he is more likely to hang around kids who will support expression of that anger. Kids, who gravitate to others just like themselves, are only hearing one point of view and are limited in their abilities to get their questions answered.

That's where we come in. We say, "Hey, there is an answer. The answer is found in God. There are some absolutes that you can hang your hat on. There is somebody who loves you. We want you to call us and tell us your story."

Humans are really created to share feelings and are far healthier when we talk things out. When people have been hurt, one of the best things they can do is keep telling their stories.

Why? There is power in tapping into the dark hole deep within the soul where pain is kept. This process brings pain to light where it can be looked at in an objective way.

The HopeLine offers young people a safe place where they can talk about their experiences.

WHAT TEENS NEED TO TELL THEIR STORIES

Teenagers must feel:

1. that you are not going to hurt them,
2. you are going to listen to their story,
3. you are going to tell them the truth,
4. you are not going to play head games.

Once kids feel you meet those conditions, there is a strong chance young people will trust you and tell you their stories.

This is what kids experience when they listen to my radio show or call the HopeLine. Obviously, the message is getting out or the calls to the HopeLine wouldn't be doubling each year.

DEALING WITH TEEN INDEPENDENCE

Teens are moving away from their parents, which is a healthy thing. Sometimes it is easier for parents to have their teens talk with somebody on the telephone with whom the family doesn't know, yet everyone feels safe. Kids do a lot of first time disclosures with us because there is anonymity.

My 15-year-old son's friend was electrocuted right in front of my son. It was terrible. I tried to help my son as best I could, but you know, he also went to his youth pastor. I welcomed that because going to a safe adult, other than parents, can be a healthy thing.

The HopeLine provides kids with a safe place to tell their stories. Dealing with feelings and "skeletons in the closet" can stop and reverse depression — no matter what the issues are. Some kids, especially boys, are taught the "don't talk, don't trust, don't feel" rules. We believe kids, especially those who have been hurt, need to talk, trust and feel.

Here is a story which illustrates the "talk, trust,

feel" point. Recently, I meet with about 20 hurt and troubled kids in a group home. The kids had come from broken or troubled homes. Most had found themselves on the wrong side of the law. Many had been so abused that they needed special attention. During my talk, I met a man in his 50's who worked helping these kids. He was a nice guy and the kids were fond of him. Shortly after the talk, a couple of kids got into a fight. The man tried to break it up and had a heart attack. He died in front of them.

Later, I spoke with one of the group home leaders, who works with these kids, about the incident. The leader commented that the kids did not show any emotion — just blank stares. If they let their emotions show over this tragedy, that would take them all the way back to the hurt which brought them to the home. By talking, trusting and feeling, those kids would have tapped into a flood of emotions.

Often, people want to avoid pain — their own and other's. If they ponder on a problem too long, then they feel obligated to do something. They may not feel they have the time, money or heart to act, so they look the other way. In some cases, people let denial alter their reality. It is very easy for adults to go into denial about young people and say, "It's too complicated. We don't know what we can do for these kids. Let's just look the other way and it will all be fine." And we do feel fine. . . until a real tragedy takes place like a suicide or school shooting. Then the cycle repeats and fear and anxiety grow.

Many problems which kids face today can be traced back through the cycle of generations. For example, studies reveal that children who have been sexually abused are more likely to be abusers. Behaviors which adults demonstrate to young people can escalate into social nightmares such as those which we face today.

WHAT TEENAGERS REALLY WANT

The fact of the matter is that teenagers are trying to find who they are as individuals. They begin to question, “Am I okay? Am I loved?”

Our relationships would be far easier if they would just say to us, “Hey, Mom and Dad, I'm going through these struggles. I don't know who I am right now. Am I still loved?”

An adult could deal with that: “Of course, we understand you are going through struggles.”

But instead, often teens become withdrawn, surly, angry, loud or disrespectful. They are asking the same question, but using inappropriate methods. So as parents we can say, “Look, I'm going to love you no matter what, but what you are doing is inappropriate. There are consequences for what you are doing. But just because there are consequences, it in no way stops the fact that I absolutely love you and will always love you."

What difference do you think it would make in young people's lives and in the world, if kids were told multiple times a day by their parents, "I love you no matter what. There are consequences for your actions, but I love you. I love you, but there are boundaries."

It would absolutely change the world. It would be so much healthier. And in time, even those who have been damaged would begin to change.

Basically, kids are asking four questions:

1. Do you love me?
2. Can I trust you?
3. Are you real?
4. Do your values work?

Young people want to know if you are real enough to get to their level. You must be caring and dedicated to understand their culture. When teenagers trust you and let you into their world, it is a tremendous compliment.

At the HopeLine, we are saying, "Let us come in. Yes, we love you. Yeah, we trust you and we can be trustworthy. Yes, we are real. We'll show you Christian values that work."

Let every man be swift to hear,
slow to speak, slow to wrath.

James 1:19

CHAPTER 19

$5 Saves A Life

Dayle Maloney

My heart broke when I heard the news about the killings at Columbine High School. The outbreak in recent school years of kids who've been killing and injuring each other has made me realize the importance of the HopeLine.

It's because of financial contributions from concerned people that the HopeLine can afford to help 120,000 kids. That's nearly double the 65,000 kids who were previously helped. HopeLine supporters can instantly see where their money has made a difference. On average the cost of a phone call is $5. Can you help one kid a month? Call your contribution in to 817-249-6000 or fax or mail it in using the "I Want To Help The Kids!" form at the back of this book.

And if you are not already involved, join Nutrition For Life which is the company with a cause. Why? To help your own family. There is a revolution taking place in North America. Adults who, at one time, placed their job first are now placing their families first. I've seen an entrepreneurial boom in home-based businesses, telecommuting and job sharing. These options give parents more time with their children. A recent study by *USA Today* revealed 66% of parents said they would accept lower pay for more time with their families.

Other parents, in fact, are choosing to stay home with their families and are making *more* money. How? By starting their own Nutrition For Life businesses from their kitchen tables or spare rooms. Most people start on a part-time basis until they have replaced their income. In addition to monthly income, Nutrition For Life offers their distributors car payments up to $3,500 per month and house payments up to $10,000 per month. People from office managers to doctors have been able to replace their incomes and stay home with their kids in as little as six to twelve months.

For more information, call the person who gave you this book. More than likely, his or her name and phone number appear on the inside of the front or back cover of this book.

CHAPTER 20

Kids Want Help

Dawson McAllister

We've learned from the Columbine incident that the teenage shooters felt as though they were outcasts. Recently, the *New York Times* reported that three out of every four kids on a high school campus felt that no one cared about them. I'm not sure what school or schools they polled, but none of our campuses should have these numbers.

Kids need a place to turn. In the wake of the school shootings, communities are trying to offer interim phone centers where kids can talk to temporary, local volunteers. Many kids are afraid to talk to people they know. Young people have told me they like the anonymity of calling a national center and talking to a person who is safely at a distance. Kids don't want to share their fears with someone who they might later discover knows their parents.

In order to guarantee that kids have someone safe to talk to, continual resources must be dedicated to finding, training and retaining volunteers. Staffing a call center is a serious, time-consuming business. The HopeLine has served thousands of North American kids since 1991, and presently is available after school and 24 hours on weekends. We have the infrastructure in place for expansion to 24 hours, 7 days a week, 365 days a year. Your donation will help us accomplish this growth.

As Dayle Maloney says, "We just have to keep going. We're going to climb the mountain one step at a time. Inch-by-inch, it's a cinch. Yard-by-yard, it's hard."

Nutrition For Life distributors are pledging at least $5 a month to the HopeLine. We're seeing pledges of $20, $50 or $100 each month — whatever people can afford. To make contributions easier for distributors, Nutrition For Life deducts the amount distributors request from their Master Card, Discover, Visa, American Express or checking account. This amount is sent directly to the HopeLine in the specific distributor's name.

People who want to contribute to the HopeLine but are not distributors of Nutrition For Life can call 817-249-6000 or fax or mail the form at the back of this book.

PART 5

LESSONS FROM LITTLETON

CHAPTER 21

Teens Teach The World

Dawson McAllister

Next you're going to read my conversations with kids about how they felt following the killings at Columbine High School. These are the transcriptions of actual phone calls I received on the *Dawson McAllister Live!* radio show the week after the Colorado tragedy. In these calls the teens did most of the talking. No one describes teen issues as well as the young people themselves. The dialogue was powerful.

You will be able to tell right away that most of the comments from these kids are highly religious — a lot about Jesus, God and their faiths. The school shootings have prompted a great deal of spiritual talk from teenagers. What they experienced was a life and death situation.

I am mindful of what United States Representative Richard Gephart said when people asked, "What laws are you going to pass to help solve teen violence?" In paraphrasing Gephart's reply, he said that the government would do the best they could, but this is an issue of the heart. In the end, kids' problems, pain and violence are spiritual issues.

The following pages are presented to you not in an attempt to change your religious beliefs. That's not the issue here. Regardless of religion, there are basic principles we can all agree on which can be applied to help kids. The following conversations were broadcast live during my radio show as teenagers shared their lessons from Littleton.

Train up a child
in the way they should go
and when they're old,
they will not depart from it.

Proverbs 22:6

CHAPTER 22

Is My School Next?

Dawson McAllister & Paula

"You know, there were so many victims of the killings in Colorado. Not simply the ones who were murdered, as tragic as that is, but the victims all across North America. Teenagers who are now scared. Teenagers who now feel overwhelmed. Almost every teenager I've talked to in North America knows somebody in their school who could pull that trigger, who could throw a bomb. It's sad because God never really intended teenagers to have to go through this, to be overwhelmed by this. The teenage years should be a carefree, happy time. Instead, many teens are wondering, 'Am I going to be the next one to get a bullet? Am I going to be dead tomorrow?' It's really upsetting. This next call is a sad call. Hi, Paula."

"Hi."

"You've been thinking about this, haven't you?"

"Yes, I have."

"And how do you feel about it?"

"Well, I'm sad because this could happen at my school. I don't want it to happen because I've got a lot of friends. I'm a very emotional person. When I was reading these articles I just started crying. I just can't believe this. This was so sad. I mean the other ones (shootings) really didn't hit me. This one hit me for some reason. I just started crying. There was one of the boys (at Littleton); his name was Dan. He was fifteen. He was shot holding the door open for other students to get out. He died on the sidewalk a few feet away from safety. His body laid outside for twenty-four hours. I cried because most people don't think about other people holding the door. They're like, "Well, I gotta get out of here for myself." He was just holding the door for other people and he got shot doing it."

"You know, it was so incredibly graphic. You know, like you said, that boy's body lying out there for 24 hours. The bodies of the students in the cafeteria, hallway and library, were in there almost 36 hours. Paula, it's enough to make anybody cry. Shocking and horrible."

"Uh-huh. I'm just trying to deal with it right now because this is tough. I feel really bad for those kids who go to that school. They're not going to have their friends with them. And I was like, whoa, this is too much for me."

Though a mighty army
marches against me,
my heart shall know no fear!
I am confident God will save me.
Psalm 27:3

CHAPTER 23

If They Only Had One Friend

Dawson McAllister and Brianne

"One of the greatest lessons which I have personally received from Littleton is how many kids feel they really are outcasts. I read in the *New York Times* where a survey was conducted on a high school campus asking students whether they felt anyone on campus cared about them. Three out of four kids answered, 'No one cares about me.'"

"Imagine the number of teenagers who are walking down the hallways of middle schools and high schools in America and Canada, and around the world, who feel that no one loves them? How many teenagers in our high schools have the outward appearance of having it together, but on the inside they're lonely, they're aching, and they're longing to be accepted by someone? And, of course, many of these kids are fair game for getting into the wrong group only because they feel that they're being accepted into that group. This next call so articulates what came through loud and clear to me. Brianne, how are you tonight?"

"Pretty good. I've been thinking about this thing in Littleton quite a bit. I guess it really kind of woke me up a bit. I wasn't actually picked on in school in the way those kids were, but I can identify with them really well. I have a strong belief that this could've been prevented if those kids had even one friend, just one friend, that let them know that they cared and that could have influenced them. I know what it feels like to go to school and honestly think that no one in school, as far as a kid was concerned, cared about what I was experiencing. It's just as humiliating to have nobody talk to you, and everybody knowing that no one's talking to you, as to be picked on physically. I just urge students to, before you look at a kid and say they're different and avoid them, think about how devastating that is to that student. They know that you're avoiding them. They know when you're being a fake. I heard (a caller) Doug talking about cliques and inner circles. I said to myself, 'Yes, exactly!' People don't think school can be a nightmare."

"Brianne, how did you break through or get over some of this hurt?"

"I still haven't. I've moved. I'm taking one class at the high school right now, but I really don't have any friends. And I guess that's why I was trying to reach out to other people who were lonely. I know what it's like to be lonely. I've been totally blind since birth. I know it's easy for a sighted student to look out over the room of kids and see somebody. Because I don't have that advantage, I'm wondering how I can find those kids who need love and acceptance and reach out to them."

"Brianne, I think it'd be gutsy, but consider having the teacher let you stand up and say, 'Hey I'm looking for friends. I can't see people who are looking for friends, but I'm here. I'd like to be your friend if you'll come up and talk to me.' I think I'd be the vulnerable one. Brianne, thanks for your beautiful call. God bless you."

"Thank you, Dawson. Bye."

Kindness is a language which the deaf can hear and the blind can see.

CHAPTER 24

People Don't Care How Much You Know, Until They Know How Much You Care

Dawson McAllister and Doug

"One of the lessons from Littleton is the age-old teaching of what happens when a certain peer group begins to fight and be cruel to another peer group, or one social class goes after another social class — them versus us. It's an age-old problem brought up-to-date: people making fun of other people, not reaching out to help others different from themselves. We've seen how that can lead to tragedy. This call makes that statement abundantly clear. Hey, Doug!"

"Hey, Dawson."

"How you doing tonight?"

"I'm doing pretty good."

"What is the lesson of Littleton to you, my man?"

"It's to be careful about how I treat others. I think it's a warning about what we say to each other. If we're gossiping about someone, if we rejected someone from our 'in' crowd because they looked a little bit different, if we are mean to people because, you know, we just can't deal with those kind of people or they're just not like us. And I think that is the main reason why we have a lot of this problem. We have our social classes and we won't let other people in. So, as a challenge, I guess you could say Jesus went out of his own social class. Whether it was just a simple fisherman, a hated tax collector, or a prostitute, Jesus went out of his social class to talk to other people and to do things with them. And so that is my challenge, God's challenge, to make sure that you're not just sticking to your own social class. That you're reaching out to other people whether they may be different or you may have a hard time being with them, still do it. And don't do it because you feel some obligation by Christ, because people will tell that. People know while you're doing it. Do it because you want to and because you want to know them and care about them."

"Doug, can you think of somebody in your school like that? Give me the first name of somebody in your school who's so much different than you. As you would say, out of your social class. Someone you feel God would want you to go and show love to?

"I'd probably have to say Ann."

"Tell me about her."

"She's a real loner. She doesn't really talk to very many people. She has just a few friends that she'll actually be with. Ann's really depressed. She likes to write poetry. Most of her poetry is about death or very sad and depressing because that's how her life feels. Nobody talks to her because they are afraid. But it's something that I try to do, when I can. I sit and talk to her in class about what she's interested in and make sure she knows that she's cared about — at least by one person."

"Is there somebody on your campus, Doug, that you're not at ease with because they're scary?

"Yeah, I'd have to say there's some of what, in our school, would be called the "freaks." I would not necessarily want to hang around them. But, I think, in Littleton and then other schools they felt that they needed to separate themselves because, as you said, three out of four people don't feel that they're cared about. Well, they felt that in their individual social class they could be cared about, so they had to protect their social class. They wouldn't reach out to other people. They had to be real closed in to their own social class because that's where they were cared about. I think that's how a lot of people are. You may think that they're scary, but they're just trying to protect themselves."

"Doug, think about some of the gangs and the scary situations people get in because they think somebody in that group cares about them. The power of somebody caring about you is incredible. And that's why we have to just really reach out and care about people."

"I guess that's the challenge or the warning I felt God led me to tell you guys about."

"Thank you, Doug. A great call. Thanks, man."

"Thank you very much."

CHAPTER 25

Teens Claim God's Promise

Dawson McAllister and Tahlia

"Every so often I get a call on my show I'll never forget. This is one of them — a call from a teenage girl from Paducah. She was involved with the slayings of three girls in 1997. If you recall, there was a prayer group of about 30 or so kids praying in the lobby of the school. After they had finished praying, this troubled young man opened fire killing three girls. Now, the girl who called in was there, has a tremendous story to tell."

"Hi, Tahlia."

"Hi, Dawson. Can I say something to the Columbine kids just really quick that are listening?

"Sure, sure."

"Right now, all of the world is watching. I mean, in 1997 all the world watched our high school. Now they're all watching you. It's so easy to serve God and to love God when all the cameras are on or whenever there's so much shock and reality really hasn't set in. But the next three or four weeks, three or four months, are going to be some of the hardest. That's when you begin to realize there are empty desks and empty podiums. That's when reality sets in. And that's when you begin to question and wonder "why." But you have to hang on because God promises that he'll pull you through. You have to stand so strong until the end. And look up scriptures about peace. Look up scriptures about joy. Memorize them. During the nights when you can't sleep, whenever you have nightmares, begin to quote those scriptures. Claim God's promise. And for all the teenagers out there who are so scared, who have heard about the girls in our school who died praying, we haven't been given a spirit of fear. God didn't give us a spirit of fear, so you can't live in that fear. You have to trust God; trust His Word. He'll be more than faithful if you just trust Him. Put your hope in Him. So that's really all I have to say. And know, Columbine, know that Paducah is mourning with you. Our prayers are with you. Know from a survivor, who was there, who saw, who held bloody hands and watched people die, know that God is faithful. God will bring you through this.

For His merciful kindness
is great towards us:
and the truth of the Lord
endeareth forever.

Psalm 117:2

CHAPTER 26

Which Path Will You Take?

Dawson McAllister and Kevin

"Another lesson from Littleton which came through loud and clear, was that the students who are hurt, who are outcasts, who are bitter or hostile, there's another way. You've got to make the right choices; you can reach out. You must reach out. You hear from kids over and over again, the 'reach out message.' Here's an eloquent 19-year-old giving that message. Hey, Kevin. How's it going for you tonight? I understand you are a first-time listener and first-time caller to our show?"

"Yes, Sir. If I could, could I just speak to the kids out there? Is that going to be a problem?"

"You can do what you want, man. It's your show."

"Kids, students, people of all ages, I know it's tough to find the love and caring you need in places. It's a weird world. But you need to take it upon yourself. Don't wait for the next guy to do it because that's not helping anything. If you're out there and you feel you have nobody that loves you, well, know that someone does. Pick up the Good Book. He cares for you and there are people out there. More people than you know care about you than you think. Just look for them. Through Him you'll find them all. I promise you that. I've been down that road."

"Kevin, how has that road been for you? What happened?"

"My parents split up when I was ten. My mother worked real hard for the government. Her hours were long and crazy. I found myself doing my own laundry at twelve years old. I'm not giving myself accolades here, by any means, but I mean I know it's rough. I had a very loving brother who was a friend and looked out for me all the time. I didn't realize that until probably a year ago. But, people are there, man. You just got to find them. You know, I chose the wrong road. Luckily, I've been swayed back off of it. There's two ways to go, kids. You can go the way the kids did at Columbine High School, and we all know that was a pretty bad idea."

"Isn't that the truth, Kevin? 'There's two ways to go' is right."

"Yeah"

"Good call, Kevin. Thanks for calling.

If you do not stand firm in your faith, you will not stand at all.

Isaiah 7:9

CHAPTER 27

I Feel Their Pain

Dawson McAllister and Debra

"One of the issues that has come forward from these Columbine killings and one of the lessons that we can certainly learn from Littleton is that there are a lot of kids walking around with a lot of hate. This call talks about hate that can be in someone's heart and how to remedy the hate. What would you like to say tonight, Debra?"

"Well, these two killers in Colorado, the strange part is, I can relate totally to them."

"Tell me about that."

"Well, I've been ridiculed a lot throughout my life — constantly beat up and teased. Just recently,

I've had an entire classroom full of people turn and laugh at me in my face. I've been called a witch and a lot of other meaner words. It's just a whole bunch of hate built up in my heart. I just got saved three weeks ago.

"Three weeks ago, Debra?"

"Yup."

"Congratulations."

"Thanks."

"Has Jesus made a difference already?"

"A big one."

"Tell me about that."

"Well, it used to be I just wished that people would die. At home I would cry because these people would talk about me so much. Now, when someone calls me a bad name, it's like, maybe I should pray for this person. It could be someone walking across the street and I say, maybe I need to pray for that person. I just pray and pray and pray. I've been asking God to take the hate out of my heart because it's still there. I don't wish people dead because it's wrong, but at the same time, people make me very angry at the things they say about me. That's how I can relate to the two boys. They've had so much hate built up in their hearts and it just consumed them. It ate them apart. That almost happened to me before Jesus came and rescued me. The Colorado thing just hit me right in the heart because someone actually died for their religion. I have to turn and ask myself, 'Could I do that?' Right now, I think I could because the reward comes in the end. It just tore me up inside because I know exactly where they're coming from. I was crying for the two boys and just apologizing to them in my heart for all these people who talked about them and ridiculed them. If they were alive today, even if they didn't like blacks, you know, because I'm black, I'd hug them and apologize for all these people talking about them. I know how it is."

"What would you say to Christian students? You were on the other side, if you will."

"Don't give up. Die for your religion if God wills you to die for Him. He has done so much for you. No matter what you do, He's always going to love you. Plus, He sent His own Son to die for you. Just return the favor. Do not give up."

CHAPTER 28

You Make A Living By What You Receive; You Make A Life By What You Give

Dayle Maloney

Folks, the lessons here are obvious. For whatever reasons, there are thousands upon thousands of teenagers who are walking around full of fear and/or hate. These kids are dangerous — dangerous to themselves, and obviously dangerous to others. But as you can also tell, there is a solution to that fear and hate. It is a spiritual solution.

Get involved immediately by helping the HopeLine reach more of these kids. Don't wait. Take the first step now.

If you are currently a Nutrition For Life distributor, call World Headquarters at 1-800-800-7377 and make your pledge today. If you are not a Nutrition For Life distributor and would like to be, call the person who gave you this book. Whether or not you are a Nutrition For Life distributor or plan on becoming one, you can always support the HopeLine with a call to 817-249-6000. Or simply use the "I Want To Help The Kids" form at the back of this book.

Stretch yourself a little bit. If $5 is what you want to give, then give $5. If you can give $10, $15 or $20, then do it. Right now, with the school tragedies that are happening, we need every penny to open those call lines 24 hours a day, 7 days a week, 365 days a year. This is a big project. When I first got involved in this project about a year ago, I thought, "Oh, no problem. This'll be a piece of cake." It's a massive project we're involved in, touching the lives of these young people. We can't do this project alone. It's bigger than we could ever possibly handle. We need your help. If everybody will just do a little bit, it's a project that'll easily be accomplished.

Nutrition For Life is going to go down in history as the company with a cause that stepped forward to help North America's young people. Together, we can say, "We made a difference for the young people of North America."

Nobody who ever gave his best regretted it.

LAST CALL FOR HELP: CHANGING NORTH AMERICA ONE TEEN AT A TIME

North American Teenagers Are In Trouble

Drugs and alcohol, pregnancy, sexual and physical abuse and neglect have left many teens numb. Their confusion and anger have led them to violent and amoral behavior. Without a "home base" for moral, emotional, psychological and spiritual direction, teenagers are now experiencing more hopelessness than ever imagined.

The HopeLine Helps

The HopeLine is a permanent help line that assists kids with every kind of issue from rape and suicide to "puppy love." Young people 21-years and under can contact the HopeLine by calling 1-800-394-HOPE.

The HopeLine currently operates on an average of 8 hours per day. Its budget will allow 65,000 kids to call and receive help. Current budget constraints force another 160,000 kids to go without help because they will have called after operating hours or received a busy signal. In one week following the Colorado school shooting, approximately 5,000 kids called the HopeLine for assistance — only a portion received the help they so desperately desired. It is estimated that next year, well over 200,000 kids will call for guidance and support.

Our goal, with your help, is to have the HopeLine available to all North American kids 24 hours a day, 7 days a week, 365 days a year.

"I WANT TO HELP THE KIDS!"

YES! Dayle and Dawson, count me as a member of your team whose purpose is to make the HopeLine available 24-hours a day, 7 days a week, 365 days a year for kids throughout North America.

I authorize the Dawson McAllister Association to deduct:

☐ $5.00 (min.) on a monthly basis -or-

☐ $____________ on a monthly basis -or-

☐ $____________ one-time

From the account indicated below:

☐ Visa ☐ Master Card ☐ American Express

☐ Discover/NOVUS ☐ Check-by-phone

☐ I am enclosing a check payable to the HopeLine.

Account # ______________________________________

Exp. Date __________________

Routing# (for check-by-phone)____________________

Name ____

NFL Dist. ID # (if applicable) ____________________

Address ____

City ____________________ St____ Zip_________

Signature ______________________________________

Phone (_________) _____________________________

Fax this form to 817-249-6009 or mail to Dawson McAllister HopeLine, PO Box 26746, 10180 Rolling Hills Dr., Benbrook, TX 76126 or call 817-249-6000.

The Dawson McAllister Association and the HopeLine are a 501(c)(3) fully tax exempt organization. All contributions are tax deductible to the fullest extent of the law.

LAST CALL FOR HELP: CHANGING NORTH AMERICA ONE TEEN AT A TIME

North American Teenagers Are In Trouble

Drugs and alcohol, pregnancy, sexual and physical abuse and neglect have left many teens numb. Their confusion and anger have led them to violent and amoral behavior. Without a "home base" for moral, emotional, psychological and spiritual direction, teenagers are now experiencing more hopelessness than ever imagined.

The HopeLine Helps

The HopeLine is a permanent help line that assists kids with every kind of issue from rape and suicide to "puppy love." Young people 21-years and under can contact the HopeLine by calling 1-800-394-HOPE.

The HopeLine currently operates on an average of 8 hours per day. Its budget will allow 65,000 kids to call and receive help. Current budget constraints force another 160,000 kids to go without help because they will have called after operating hours or received a busy signal. In one week following the Colorado school shooting, approximately 5,000 kids called the HopeLine for assistance — only a portion received the help they so desperately desired. It is estimated that next year, well over 200,000 kids will call for guidance and support.

Our goal, with your help, is to have the HopeLine available to all North American kids 24 hours a day, 7 days a week, 365 days a year.

"I WANT TO HELP THE KIDS!"

YES! Dayle and Dawson, count me as a member of your team whose purpose is to make the HopeLine available 24-hours a day, 7 days a week, 365 days a year for kids throughout North America.

I authorize the Dawson McAllister Association to deduct:

☐ $5.00 (min.) on a monthly basis -or-

☐ $____________ on a monthly basis -or-

☐ $____________ one-time

From the account indicated below:

☐ Visa ☐ Master Card ☐ American Express

☐ Discover/NOVUS ☐ Check-by-phone

☐ I am enclosing a check payable to the HopeLine.

Account # ________________________________

Exp. Date ________________

Routing# (for check-by-phone)____________________

Name ____

NFL Dist. ID # (if applicable) ____________________

Address ______________________________________

City ____________________ St____ Zip__________

Signature ____________________________________

Phone (_________) ____________________________

Fax this form to 817-249-6009 or mail to Dawson McAllister HopeLine, PO Box 26746, 10180 Rolling Hills Dr., Benbrook, TX 76126 or call 817-249-6000.

The Dawson McAllister Association and the HopeLine are a 501(c)(3) fully tax exempt organization. All contributions are tax deductible to the fullest extent of the law.

LAST CALL FOR HELP: CHANGING NORTH AMERICA ONE TEEN AT A TIME

North American Teenagers Are In Trouble

Drugs and alcohol, pregnancy, sexual and physical abuse and neglect have left many teens numb. Their confusion and anger have led them to violent and amoral behavior. Without a "home base" for moral, emotional, psychological and spiritual direction, teenagers are now experiencing more hopelessness than ever imagined.

The HopeLine Helps

The HopeLine is a permanent help line that assists kids with every kind of issue from rape and suicide to "puppy love." Young people 21-years and under can contact the HopeLine by calling 1-800-394-HOPE.

The HopeLine currently operates on an average of 8 hours per day. Its budget will allow 65,000 kids to call and receive help. Current budget constraints force another 160,000 kids to go without help because they will have called after operating hours or received a busy signal. In one week following the Colorado school shooting, approximately 5,000 kids called the HopeLine for assistance — only a portion received the help they so desperately desired. It is estimated that next year, well over 200,000 kids will call for guidance and support.

Our goal, with your help, is to have the HopeLine available to all North American kids 24 hours a day, 7 days a week, 365 days a year.

"I WANT TO HELP THE KIDS!"

YES! Dayle and Dawson, count me as a member of your team whose purpose is to make the HopeLine available 24-hours a day, 7 days a week, 365 days a year for kids throughout North America.

I authorize the Dawson McAllister Association to deduct:

☐ $5.00 (min.) on a monthly basis -or-

☐ $__________ on a monthly basis -or-

☐ $__________ one-time

From the account indicated below:

☐ Visa ☐ Master Card ☐ American Express

☐ Discover/NOVUS ☐ Check-by-phone

☐ I am enclosing a check payable to the HopeLine.

Account # ______________________________

Exp. Date ______________

Routing# (for check-by-phone)________________

Name ________________________________

NFL Dist. ID # (if applicable) ________________

Address ______________________________

City ________________ St____ Zip________

Signature ______________________________

Phone (________) ________________________

Fax this form to 817-249-6009 or mail to Dawson McAllister HopeLine, PO Box 26746, 10180 Rolling Hills Dr., Benbrook, TX 76126 or call 817-249-6000.

The Dawson McAllister Association and the HopeLine are a 501(c)(3) fully tax exempt organization. All contributions are tax deductible to the fullest extent of the law.